PLAN AND PRE
SURVIVING THE ZOMBIE
APOCALYPSE

Congratulations on purchasing **Plan and Prep: Surviving the Zombie Apocalypse**. This book will serve as an easy to understand guide for preparation and planning for emergency and disaster events that you may encounter in your lifetime.

No matter your geographic location, age, race, financial situation or religious or political affiliation…you CAN be affected by emergencies and disasters. Those that plan and prepare accordingly will not always fare better than those that don't, but certainly if given the chance to survive an event, the prepared individual will usually stand a much better chance.

There are many books that have been written that follow the trials and tribulations of people placed into survival situations. There are stories of people forced to eat things that no human should ever have to eat, removing their own body parts, starving, dehydrating and even suffering wounds from attacks of wild animals or criminal assaults.

Unfortunately, or fortunately depending on how you view the glass of water, there has never been a Zombie Apocalypse from which to draw experience or knowledge. For this reason all survival techniques, television shows, movies, books, etc are written using basic survival techniques that are universal in nature. One thing is always missing however, planning and preparation.

Have you ever seen a movie about someone that planned and prepared for a Zombie Apocalypse? No you haven't, because it's never happened, at least to my knowledge. Everything has focused on how people are coping with life after Zombies and they all talk about how they were school teachers or nurses or garbage collectors and never thought anything like this could ever happen.

Imagine how the story arc changes when you introduce a character that has been planning and preparing for such an event. First of all, they are commonly referred to as crazy, strange, weird or nuts. If you openly discuss your opinion that "something bad" is likely to happen in the future you are labeled a "Doomsayer" or worse. Suddenly you find yourself lumped into a category of people that require careful monitoring and people tell their children to stay away from your house or your family. Well, up until a few years ago that is…..

Thirty years ago people would have thought you were crazy to read a book about a zombie apocalypse. Twenty years ago the book would have been accepted as entertainment, but not taken seriously in any format. Ten years ago a few people would have nodded their heads and started asking questions about it while most still dismissed it. Today, people are actively seeking out answers to questions posed on the possibility of zombies and books on planning and preparation for other events are gaining much momentum.

Although this book does focus some material on a Zombie Apocalypse, this is used mainly to demonstrate a "worst case scenario" event. This event could have easily been replaced with a global thermonuclear war, abrupt global climate change or even an alien invasion; the results would still be the same in many regards.

The truth of the matter is this; it does not matter what type of disaster befalls you or your family, planning and preparation will give you a much better chance of survival than you would have if you don't plan at all. Just because you are prepared does NOT mean you are looking forward to using your plans.

Remember the mantra: Hope for the best, but prepare for the worst.

Foreword:

This guide is meant to provide valuable information for emergency preparation. It should be understood however that there are many factors and situations that cannot be listed as the scope is entirely too large. Discriminating factors include everything from season/time of year to local climate, survival experience of the reader, age and number of children, financial situation, length of the event and many other aspects. Obviously not every aspect can be covered in this guide.

Planning and preparation are vital to successfully surviving in any environment, but you must also remember that training is also extremely important. Training incorporates practice as well as learning. Planning that you will trap animals with a snare is easy, you just plan it; performing those actions may be a lot harder once you try to do it though, so make sure you train and practice.

This guide is a common sense reference for anyone. You don't need military or survival training to complete any of the things listed in this book.

As a "guide" this book provides you with the subjects you will need to learn and the tasks you will need to master in order to successfully plan and prepare for serious events.

THIS IS NOT AN INSTRUCTION MANUAL. THIS GUIDE IS MEANT TO ASSIST YOU WITH DECIDING WHAT YOU NEED TO HAVE, KNOW AND DO TO PREPARE FOR A SERIOUS EVENT. INDIVIDUAL INSTRUCTION ON ITEMS, USAGE, SKILLS AND THEORIES WILL NEED TO BE RESEARCHED BY THE READER.

Copyright © 2012 by Alex Newton
All rights reserved.
ISBN-13: 978-2475011170
ISBN-10: 2475011173

ALL RIGHTS RESERVED. This book contains material protected under International and Federal Copyright Laws and Treaties. Any unauthorized reprint or use of this material is prohibited. No part of this book may be reproduced or transmitted in any form or by any means, electronic or mechanical, including photocopying, recording, or by any information storage and retrieval system without express written permission from the author / publisher.

Table of Contents

FOREWORD: 4

Emergencies and Disasters 12
   EMERGENCIES 12
      Bill's House Burns Down 13
   DISASTERS 15
      Bill Gets Prepared 16
      Evacuation Planning 16
      Bill's Bug Out Bag (BoB) 18
      Family Planning 20
      Planning Ahead 28
      Bugging In versus Bugging Out 28
   BILL WEATHERS A FLASH FLOOD 32
   BILL SURVIVES A PANDEMIC 35
      Evacuation 39
      The Aftermath 41

Zombie Apocalypse 44
   COULD IT HAPPEN? 44
      Hollywood versus Reality 44
   BILL TAKES ON THE ZOMBIES 49
      April Fool's 50
      Zombie Day (Z Day) 51
      Z Day +1 56
      Living Apart 56
      Surviving….Thriving 57
      After the Zombie Flu 58

Real World Zombies 59
   The Catalyst 60
   The Reality 61

The Cure	61

Survival Basics 66
PREPARATION 66
Geographic Concerns 67
Food & Water 69
Health and Welfare 73
Weapons / Protection 75
Stockpiling 77
Primary Shelter Site (PSS) 81
Operational Security (Op Sec) 86
How do I….? 89
THE EVENT 91
Moving to your PSS 91
Mob Rules 91
The Price of Tea In China 92
AFTERMATH 93
Community Rules 93
Building Your Community 96
MAJOR EVENTS THAT REQUIRE PREPARATION 101
Quite Likely 101
Not As Likely 103

The Real Apocalypse 105
SOONER OR LATER 105
Root Cause 105
Air is Rare 106
Mobile Society in the Western US 106
Communal Society in the Midwest US 107
Northern and Northeastern US 108

Appendix A 110
SURVIVAL TIPS AND TRICKS 110

    Primitive Fire Building 110
    Finding Water 111
    Water Filtering 112
    Snaring a Meal 114
    Keep Your Gas Tank ½ Full 115
    Get Gas from a Vehicle 115
    Sleeping on the Run 115
    Add Meat and Chicken to Your Diet 116
    Preventive Maintenance 116
    Super Glue for Cuts 116
    Cauterize a Wound using a Bullet 116
    Make Soap from Animal Fat 117
DON'T KILL YOURSELF 118
    Dehydration 118
    Cook Your Food Thoroughly 118
    Boil Your Water 119
    Aim for the Head….NOT! 119
    Guns are Dangerous 119
    Eco Living 119

Appendix B 120
    STATISTICAL DATA 120

Appendix C 121
    LINKS AND INFO 121

Zombie Games: 122
    ZOMB BOWLING: 123
    ZOMB JARTS: 124
    WHACK-A-ZOMB: 125

For my wife, Sara, where we're going, we don't need roads…

For my children; Kieran, Charlie and Bristol…thank you for reminding me that life isn't always serious.

For my mother, Jan, thank you for being a constant source of inspiration and helping me realize my creative potential.

Special thanks go to Jamie Mathieson, for providing all of the artwork within this book, including its wonderful cover.

You can see more of Jamie's work on the following website.

www.jamiemathiesonart.com

I have thoroughly enjoyed working with Jamie and recommend his work highly. You can find more samples of his work in the Art Showcase at the end of this book.

Emergencies and Disasters

Emergencies

Many people think they know what emergencies are and how they should handle them. In case of fire, call the fire department....in case of criminal activity, call the police department....in case of sickness, call the doctor/hospital/ambulance, etc.

For the past 20+ years most people have been able to pick up the phone and call 911 to reach professionals trained to handle just about any situation, or to provide guidance on where to seek help. The first responders that answer the calls to 911 can assist with a multitude of issues. This single call puts you into the hands of a professional dispatcher that can usually not only give you some direction but can also get the proper response started from either the fire station, police station, hospital, etc. Besides calling 911, what would you try to take with you in case of a house fire? What would you do if no one answered the phone at the 911 center?

Bill's House Burns Down

Bill Jones is sleeping when he is abruptly awakened by the shrill beep of the fire alarm. He jumps from his bed and looks at the clock, which reads 2:30am. Bill yells "What the hell?!" as he runs downstairs to find the source of the alarm, leaving his frightened wife in the bedroom.

As Bill reaches the downstairs den he sees flames and smells smoke. Realizing this is beyond his capacity to control he races back upstairs and yells to his wife and kids "The house is on fire, we have to leave!"

In a panic Bill and the family run back down the stairs, grabbing the car keys and his cell phone on the way. As they sit in the car across the street Bill's wife calls 911 while the kids watch the house become fully engulfed in flames. Relieved to have escaped the fire, it will be only minutes before Bill and his wife realize their predicament.

In their haste and lack of preparation, they have left their home in their pajamas, with no money, no identification, no insurance information and no family members to lean on. Not being prepared has now caused this family to rely on the charity of friends, strangers and the local community to provide them with everything they need until they can get access to their bank accounts, credit cards, etc.

It will be months before they get moved into a new home. The children have no clothes for school, the parents no clothes for work. Since they have no credit cards or debit cards they cannot purchase things like toothbrushes, shoes, food or even a hotel room for the night. Ultimately the insurance company will pay to replace the household items and provide money to replace necessities, but not tonight. Unless Bill or his wife has a friend they can stay with, they will watch their children spend a very frightening evening sleeping in their car or in a shelter.

This could have been avoided.

If Bill had prepared his family ahead of time with emergency evacuation drills, proper Bug Out Bag planning and a prepared "Life Folder", he and the family could ride out this event with relative ease compared to what they are about to go through. If Bill had packed a Bug Out Bag he would have access to a decent amount of cash, as well as credit cards or even a debit card. Even without a Bug Out Bag, emergency planning would have conditioned Bill to ensure his wallet was among the items he grabbed on his way out of the house in an emergency.

Although a house fire is extremely destructive and difficult to deal with, imagine how much worse things would be if this were not a personal event. Imagine this occurring on a community level due to a plane crash, train crash, sewer gas explosion, heating gas explosion, flood, etc. Imagine how the local resources would be taxed if not one family, but 50 or 100 families were all fleeing their homes and calling 911. If none of those families are prepared it places even more strain on the local community, whereas for every prepared family, it reduces the community strain drastically.

Disasters

Disasters are emergencies on steroids. Generally when you talk about a disaster it is an event that has affected an entire community/region/populace or it is an event involving mass casualties. Good examples of disasters are plane crashes, train crashes, meteor/asteroid impact, tsunami, earthquake etc. Each of these events would elicit a different response based on the size and type of the event as well as the cause of the event. If you lived in an area where a plane crashed due to mechanical failure you would most likely react differently than if the plane was brought down intentionally by terrorists, i.e. September 11th.

Local resources and first responders are much more likely to become overwhelmed in a disaster, especially in rural areas. Small town or county authorities would be required to draw resources from adjacent communities, thinning the ranks of available resources for other duties such as law enforcement, fire protection, etc. The disaster itself would command so much of the attention that crime in the area may see a drastic increase in the interim.

The other major difference between an Emergency and a Disaster is that in many cases disasters have the potential to have long term affects or even progressively worsening affects. In the event that you are near a disaster area, you may be fine initially but then be forced to evacuate or flee as the situation worsens, the affected area increases or more is discovered about the cause or nature of the event.

In Bill's case a single structure was on fire. If we had carried that example forward we would find in most cases that Bill and his family survived the event with minor difficulty, although I am sure their emergency planning will get a significant facelift. Bill's neighbors would most likely pay more attention to fire hazards for a short period, but eventually old habits will win out and the status quo will return.

In the event of a disaster, the phone call to 911 may have gone unanswered. As Bill and his wife began driving out of their neighborhood they may have seen multiple houses in flames, cars crashed and burning, people fleeing wildly through the streets, or even standing in their front yard with a weapon to defend their property. There could have been gunshots, screams, flames and many other things that quickly ignite the human fight or flight reactions.

Bill's children could have become overly frightened and began yelling or crying uncontrollably while Bill's wife might turn to him with questions like "What's going on, Bill?", "What now, Bill?" or "Where do we go,

Bill?". She isn't trying to bother her husband or overburden him; it is simply a normal reaction to turn to your "leader" in these situations for guidance. As Bill is not prepared and has not done any planning, he would be at a loss for any ideas and have to make his decisions in haste. There would be a good chance that their survival would depend on the charity of others; hopefully they could find that charity quickly.

Bill Gets Prepared

Evacuation Planning

When planning for potential evacuation due to emergency or disaster make sure to consider the following:

1) Plan a known and accessible "Rally Point" in case all family members are not home when the evacuation is enacted. This rally point should be a location enroute to your intended destination and away from congested or highly used areas.

2) Plan separate evacuation routes for your home, neighborhood, city and region.

3) Have at least two evacuation plans for your home and your city.

4) Have a specific destination, as well as a backup destination.

5) Practice your evacuation routes and determine the time required to complete each route at different times of the day.

6) Avoid areas that will quickly become saturated or areas that have the potential to become choke points. Ensure that you know which side streets are dead ends or go over water or through tunnels. Avoid these areas as they are very likely choke points, or even ambush sites in a prolonged scenario.

7) If you are driving, maintain at least one car length between yourself and the car ahead of you at all stop signs and lights. Pay very close attention to your exit lanes and watch your blind spots for people approaching your vehicle on foot.

8) If you are a city dweller remember that LOTS of people will be trying to get to the highway, causing traffic jams. Use surface roads to get out of the dense population areas and plan to enter the highway in rural areas if at all.

9) Use code words or phrases to indicate your different plans. Simply stating "It's time for us to bug out and save ourselves from the horrible death everyone else is about to encounter" may not be the best way to handle it.

10) If possible it is a wise decision to have a personal storage site between your home and your PSS, such as a storage locker. If you do decide to go this route ensure it is an outdoor facility that you can access 24/7. Store medical supplies, non-perishable food supplies, water, batteries, ammunition (if allowed), spare tires for your primary vehicle, tools, etc. Bad things happen, be prepared.

Bill's Bug Out Bag (BoB)

One preparation tool that Bill has learned is vital is a Bug Out Bag (BoB). The design of the BoB is to give you a pre-packed bag that you can grab on your way out of your home in case of emergency. The bag should have the proper supplies to get you through 3 days without resupplying.

The BoB is not a "survival" pack so much as a "bridge" pack to get you through a rough patch. The goal is to use the BoB system to sustain you while you travel from wherever you are to a designated shelter site that should already have supplies. Understand this is NOT a long term survival pack.

After carefully considering his needs, Bill has decided on the makeup of his pack:

- Water (6 Bottles)
- Flashlight / batteries
- First Aid Kit
- Personal Hygiene Kit
- Local area map and compass
- Copies of important papers
- Multi-Tool
- Change of clothes
- Cash/Credit/ID
- Snacks
- Deck of Cards

Quickly you can see that Bill's "BoB" is NOT meant for long term survival or harsh elements. This type of bag is used for "Bugging In" (aka Bedding Down) or short term dislocation from home. If Bill would have had a bag like this when his house fire occurred the family would have been much better off than they found themselves. It is a very good idea to pack a BoB in this manner and have a secondary bag packed with items for extended evacuations or larger scale disasters packed and ready as well.

Family Planning

Each family member should pack an individual Bug Out Bag. This will be kept in a specific location and updated regularly. Children tend to pack more than they should, so monitor this and ensure they understand the importance of limiting their items to the essentials.

Each family member should have a Personal Life Folder. This is vital in case of emergency. Many people will skip this portion of planning with the theory that this will create a security problem for their family member if the information is found by someone nefarious. In reality, especially if you have children, this specific item could not only save your child's life, it could also reunite you if your child is lost.

Imagine your child getting injured and being unable to communicate or unconscious. If you are not there to tell people what the child's medical conditions are they will be taking serious risks when treating the child. When I was young it was determined that I was allergic to Demerol, if I injure myself and require sedation one of the more highly utilized pain killers is Demerol, and it would kill me. With a proper Life Folder in my possession my allergy can be determined and a different route of treatment can be found.

The truth is that this information is no big secret and will not hurt your security. Better safe than sorry, just make sure you secure the information to protect it against being lost.

Kid's Bug Out Bag

- Change of clothes (x3)
- Flashlight
- Favorite toy(s)
- Blanket/Pillow
- Canteen of water
- Toilet Paper (x1)
- Personal Hygiene Kit
- Snacks
- Kid's Life Folder
- Walkie Talkie (if given to all family members)
- Batteries

Kid's Life Folder

- Recent Picture
- Name
- Age
- Address
- Parent's Names (Kid's Sheet Only)
- Parent's Contact Information
- Known Allergies or Medical Conditions
- Blood Type

Adult Bug Out Bag (Personal)

- Change of Clothes (x3)
- Canteen of Water
- Medications
- Food Rations (3 days)
- First Aid Kit
- Personal Hygiene Kit
- Toilet Paper (x1)
- Adult Life Folder (Individual)
- Knife
- Flashlight
- Walkie Talkie (if given to all family members)

Adult Life Folder (Personal)

- Personal Information Sheet
    - Recent Picture
    - Name
    - Age
    - Address
    - Known Allergies or Medical Conditions
    - Blood Type
    - Medications
    - Emergency Contact Information

Lastly there should be a "Family Bug Out Bag" and a "Family Life Folder". The family life folder will include a copy of each family member's Personal Information Sheet as well as COPIES of other important documents. Keep the Life Folders in a fireproof safe under normal circumstances to avoid loss or damage.

> ** NOTE **
>
> The Family Bug Out Bag is also commonly referred to as an **INCH** (I'm Not Coming Home) bag. This is the bag that you will use to carry everything you are going to need to get to your primary or secondary shelter site. The items in the following table are necessities that I believe every INCH bag should include, and this would be at a minimum.

I cannot stress enough the importance of the Life Folder. Although this idea is not completely new to disaster prep, it has never gotten much attention. I am hoping that with this book I can change the impression that the Life Folder is a security breach and not necessary. The truth of the matter is that in the face of an emergency or disaster I would rather run the risk of some form of ID theft than leave my children unprotected and without a means of being located. Just because you are prepared doesn't mean you will survive. It is a harsh reality that you may die and leave your children to fend for themselves or to find assistance from someone else. Having this information will be of great value to someone that has your children's best interests in mind.

Family Bug Out Bag

Flashlight (Solar/Crank)	Emergency Blankets	Glow Sticks
Hand Crank Radio	Rope/Cord 550 Para	Signal Mirror
Fire starting materials	Compass and Local Map	Ziploc Bags
Personal Hygiene	Water Purification Tabs	Batteries (Misc)
Anti-Diarrhea Meds	Rigid Water Containers	Deck of Cards
Mess Kit	Knife (camping, hunting)	Cash/Coins
Hand Sanitizer	Multi-tool	Ponchos
Canteen (steel)	Folding Shovel	Tarp
Clothing (subdued)	Camp Axe	Food Rations (MRE)
Collapsible Bucket	Survival Handbook	Can Opener
Bug repellent	Duct Tape	Sunblock

Family Life Folder

- Personal Information Sheet (One for each family member)
- Copies of each family member's SS Cards
- Copies of Life, Home, Auto Insurance Cards
- Copies of Driver's Licenses
- Copy of Last Will and Testament
- Passports
- Contact information for Next of Kin

Planning Ahead

Bill began his planning by teaching his family about Bug Out Bags and Life Folders. He talked to each family member individually and made sure that they understood exactly what he meant when he used those terms and also made sure that the kids knew this was planning for an event that he hoped would never happen. He took great care in assuring that his young children were not scared by the concept of planned evacuation and that they understood the benefits. Bill devised several games for his children to play in regards to determining what should be in their bags and how quickly they could get them and be at the Home Egress Point (HEP). Keeping the process interesting for children is sometimes difficult. Every child is different so determining the best way to approach your children with this information is vital.

** NOTE **

Remember when doing your planning and procurement to do so quietly and without bringing attention to yourself. If your neighbors know of your plans or that you have supplies on hand, you will be the first person they think of when an emergency occurs. They will remember what they saw you with and they may come and try to take it, either by asking or by force. We will cover more on this topic in the Op Sec section.

Bugging In versus Bugging Out

One of the most difficult decisions a person will have to make is the decision to either Bug In (shelter in place) or Bug Out. The decision on when to do either of these things should be fluid and based on several different criteria.

Type of Event

Natural disasters, terrorist attacks, pandemic flu outbreaks and just about every other emergency will call for a different response.

For example, if you live in downtown Chicago and there is a terrorist attack involving suicide bombers and gunfire, bugging in would most likely be the best solution. This would limit your exposure to the threat and you could be reasonably sure that the attack would not last for any extreme duration.

On the other hand, if you live in downtown Chicago and the news breaks that there is an imminent threat of nuclear attack in the city by terrorists, immediately bugging out would be your best option for long term survival.

Finally, if there is word that a pandemic virus is rampaging through the city and people are dropping dead like flies, bugging in until the initial wave of pandemonium passes and then bugging out in the aftermath may be a good idea. This would limit your exposure to the civil unrest of massive amounts of people freaking out, limit your exposure to the virus itself and provide you with a better option of getting a clear run at a safe zone. This option does have risks however. Bugging in for too long can bring you into contact with scavengers and marauders when you venture out, or when they find your home. This option could also see you trapped in your home if you wait too long and the military quarantines your area.

Simply put, your plans must include all of the above options with very flexible guidelines in order to achieve maximum effectiveness. Setting concrete markers to determine when you bug in or bug out could very easily cost you and your family their lives.

Don't misinterpret this point. PLAN AND PREPARE. Drill your evac routes and practice loading your vehicle and following those routes. Understand the types of disasters that could befall you and discuss them with your adult counterparts or significant others so that you all are on the same page if something happens. Remember though, these events become very fluid once they are set into motion and failure to have the flexibility to react can be fatal.

Geographic Location

If you are currently living in a large city, bugging in may be necessary in some cases, but ultimately getting out of the city should be your goal. Long term events will not improve the city dweller's situation at all. If you are in the suburbs of a large city you will have more time to make your decision, but you still shouldn't waste too much time.

For those people lucky enough to live in a small town or out in the country, bugging in may actually make sense. If your current location is defensible, with ample resources for food production and water, then you find yourself in a much better situation than most.

Also consider the time of year if you live in an area that suffers weather extremes such as mountains that get heavy snowfall amounts in the winter or a desert that suffers extreme drought in the summer. If you cannot survive these extremes without severe hardship or potential death, bugging out should be in the plans.

Level of Planning

If you are new to emergency and disaster planning, or have not completed your plans, this can seriously impact your decision to bug out or bug in. It would be very difficult to leave your home and travel to an unsecured or unsupplied safe point with any hope of survival if your plans are not in order. This is not to say that it cannot be done, or that you need to have a finished plan in order to take action. What this means is that when you are doing your planning you should set small and attainable goals that will assist you in your survival. Perhaps set a goal of three days worth of food and water in your home and two weeks worth in your remote location, then work up from there, setting goals as you go. Don't try to prepare your bug in location to completion before ever starting your remote location planning, this eliminates an entire survival alternative immediately.

Start with the absolute necessities, food and water. From there you can move to security items, first aid and medical care items and survival tools. Once you have managed this to a decent level you can begin looking at longer term solution materials and ideas like seeds for gardens, ammo stores, water filtration and purification, power production and consumption and techniques for gardening, hunting, trapping, etc.

Beginning this journey of preparation will not start for most people by buying a country house and filling it with guns and ammo, it will start with small purchases, like a backpack an MRE and a first aid kit. From that point where you go is up to you.

Family Matters

One very big part of making life or death decisions will be based on your responsibilities to others. Single people with no ties can easily pack up and take off, parents of small children can't do this.

Factoring small children into your emergency and disaster planning presents specific challenges. Generally speaking, the smaller the children, the more difficult the planning. I won't spend a lot of time on this subject, just understand that small children will have a much lower tolerance for temperature extremes, dehydration, malnutrition and other difficulties you may face. At the same time, smaller children may require more resources, such as bottles, diapers, formula, etc.

Older children can be an advantage if properly trained and mature enough to grasp the situation. Many people immediately start training the children in security, firearms and hunting, which isn't a bad thing at all. That being said I would suggest rounding off that training with skills such as gardening, engineering (water filtration, power production, etc) and first aid. Everyone should know how to cook and clean, as well as how to treat minor wounds.

Older family members can pose some of the same issues as small children. Many times they are incapable of tasks to assist daily routines or security, and they utilize more resources as they grow older. If your emergency plans will include older family members you will need to take into consideration their medicinal needs and the shelf life of those items as well as hygiene needs, dietary needs and the manpower to oversee these challenges. Also take into consideration their locomotion capabilities in case you need to move quickly.

In regards to children and the elderly I am not in any way advocating leaving them out of your planning or making plans to "not include" them, by whatever means. Just the opposite, I am simply pointing out that these things need to be carefully considered in all aspects of your planning.

False Alarms are Not Good

If you are like me you have a regular job, and that job pays your bills and keeps you fed and sheltered. Also if you are like me, disappearing from work suddenly for a few days will most likely cause you to lose your job. Your boss will probably react negatively when you call him up and say "I'm bugging out because of the flu" and then a week or two later you are begging for your job back after he has spent all that time working harder to pick up the lost productivity.

Also along the same vein, most people aren't going to be logging into the online banking systems and paying their bills while they are hunkered down awaiting the end of the world. If the end doesn't come, all of those bills will certainly make you think you might have been better off if it did.

Ensure you know the risks when you walk away from your ordinary life. If you are "not sure" that you should be bugging out, sit and think about it for a few minutes and run through the possibilities. Try to determine if you are willing to place your family in danger by not bugging out, but also if you are willing to place your financial future in danger if you bug out too soon.

Bill Weathers a Flash Flood

It's been one year since a fire destroyed the home of Bill Jones and his family. Since that time Bill has taken a much more active stance on emergency preparation. Bill has created emergency evacuation plans for the new house and has set up a "Bug Out Bag" (BoB) with emergency essentials. Although he wanted to do more preparation and planning, he has succumbed to the pressure of his friends and some family members calling him names and saying he was over reacting or being a doomsayer.

At 8:15PM the Emergency Broadcast System announces an evacuation order for the area in which Bill is now residing. Bill turns to his family and says "Okay guys, Code Red, Plan A, let's go!"

The first part of this announcement, "Code Red" indicates to the family members that a dangerous event is currently underway, requiring immediate action. Had Bill exclaimed "Code Green" everyone would have known that Bill was announcing a need to get things together, but that there was time available to check and double-check all of their items, add or remove things based on the "Plan" letter, get a snack and a drink to take with them and make use of the bathroom prior to hitting the road. The second part of the announcement "Plan A", indicated that the family will be initiating their primary evacuation plan. If that plan were determined to be unusable, Bill would have announced "Plan B" or even "Plan C" in order to let everyone know which of their backup plans was being activated. The reasoning behind the use of codes and plan letters is to keep anyone within earshot from knowing what is happening, which is covered in the Operational Security section.

Within 2 minutes of Bill making the Code and Plan announcement each member of the family is at the designated egress point with their own individual BoB. Bill and the family are able to successfully evacuate the home knowing that they are prepared for a short displacement.

As Bill and the family drive down the street heading for a predetermined relocation site, neighbors and friends are scrambling around their homes as mothers try to find family pictures and heirlooms that must be saved and children stand in hallways crying. Teenage kids are gathering laptops and mp3 players and dads are standing at the garage door screaming for everyone to get in the car.

Throughout this chaos the unprepared families are gathering things that they don't need and leaving behind things that may prove vital. As they drive out of the neighborhood Nick asks his father why none of their neighbors are leaving their houses. Bill replies by telling Nick that although they all received the same notice, some people will not leave. Other people, he explains, are not prepared and are trying to leave but they don't know what to bring and what to leave behind, just as they don't know where they are going to go.

When the neighbors are finally ready to leave their homes, precious time has elapsed and they find themselves stuck in a traffic jam in their own subdivision, while everyone tries in vain to move as fast as they can, no one goes anywhere. Lives are placed in needless danger when the flash flood hits the neighborhood.

At the hotel Bill watches the news and learns that several people have perished in the flash flood by being caught in a traffic jam in low lying areas, trying to pass through a short tunnel that flooded, and also crossing small rivers that overflowed the roadway and carried their vehicles into deeper water. As he watches, he realizes that as the people stuck in traffic were being swept away, he was driving up a nearly vacant road to higher ground, and a bypass out of the flood zone.

Bill gathers his family around him and shows them the cost of being unprepared. Although the family is sad that others perished, they are happy to be alive and have learned that planning holds vast advantages over its alternative. Upon returning to his home Bill volunteered to work on the cleanup efforts and once the remains of those unlucky enough to die in the event were cleared, he made sure to involve Nick in the cleanup in order to give him some extra perspective. It will be a few months before the neighborhood in which they live returns to normal. Several houses were destroyed by the flooding, although the Jones family was lucky enough not to be counted in that statistic.

This event has also tweaked Sara's interest in being prepared and she and Bill spend the next few months augmenting their already extensive emergency plans and deciding it's time to really take the possibility of a massive event seriously.

Bill Survives a Pandemic

It's been three years since a fire destroyed the home of Bill Jones and his family. Since that time Bill has taken a much more active stance on emergency preparation. Bill has created emergency evacuation plans for the new house and has set up a "Bug Out Bag" (BoB) with emergency essentials. Even in the face of criticism from friends and family, Bill has endured and carried on admirably. He has stocked goods and items, made plans and drilled his family on their roles and responsibilities.

For the past few days the news reports have been getting steadily worse. People around the world have been falling ill and dying of a new form of H5N1 Bird Flu.

Two weeks into the outbreak the virus has reached pandemic levels. Schools in the United States have been closed down and businesses have been told to send their workers home. There is no vaccine yet, but the CDC is working fast to develop one.

As the death toll begins to climb, the citizens of the United States have gone into "survival mode". Initially there were isolated reports of theft and an occasional assault, but within days this escalated to rioting, looting and general anarchy in the streets. Fire and Police were overrun and the National Guard was activated. Grocery stores were looted and picked clean within just a few days and gas stations ran dry before most people thought to check their tank. Regular citizens wander through neighborhoods and stores trying to claim the last of the leftover supplies that may have been missed. The small amount of food deliveries that are still being made are not enough to keep up with demand and are increasingly hijacked or "rerouted" to other areas.

Four weeks into the outbreak the CDC still has no vaccine. Globally there have been over 500,000 deaths. As the virus continues its march across the planet the public has lost all faith that a cure can be found. All non-essential travel has been stopped and for those that have never planned for an event of this nature, things are not looking good.

Supply lines from warehouses and ports in the western US that keep supermarkets flowing with food have now completely stopped. Large cities are no longer receiving food, medicine and other necessities. Critical infrastructure employees are being told to stay home and rolling blackouts are becoming common as power plants work on skeleton crews. The National Guard passes out food rations daily in as many places as possible, but the amount available is getting smaller and the citizens are getting less cooperative by the hour.

The virus has no political motivation, no rules to its behavior. Rich and poor alike fall to the bug. Policemen, firemen and soldiers are all susceptible and their numbers are thinned on a daily basis. After weeks of fighting a losing battle in the nation's hospitals and emergency camps, doctors and nurses are ordered to evacuate the infected areas and are placed in quarantine. Once cleared of infection they will be housed in undisclosed locations and utilized as first responders and medical staff to the nation's financial, political and military leaders. This is a construct of "Continuity of Government". Although most doctors and nurses will continue the fight until ordered to withdraw, many will consider the duty to their family as paramount and leave the front lines early.

After the orders are given to remove the medical personnel, the cities will be lost until a vaccine can be found. At this point attempting to quarantine the sick into specific areas will no longer be viable, and the quarantines will switch to life saving operations for those that are not ill, and are deemed vital to the continuity of government. Martial Law will inevitably follow, with a temporary lifting of the Posse Comitatus Act.

Eight weeks into the pandemic the global death toll has topped 20 million. Governments of the world are being pressured to produce a vaccine without the proper testing protocols being observed. This could lead to vaccinated individuals dying, having allergic reactions or even developing long term illness or disease. In the long run this could lead to reproductive issues or genetic problems. Another potential outcome is that the vaccine doesn't work. Yet even with this possibility, Hospitals are being ransacked and medical staff murdered for the small amount of supplies left.

Families are being told over loudspeaker to place their deceased loved ones in the front yard for disposal and anyone caught outside at night is subject to arrest. Lethal force has been authorized for maintaining the safety of police and military units, but this generally does not extend very far into the cities as they have become dangerous even to law enforcers.

There are no more food deliveries, no more rations, no more electricity and no more social services. Scavengers move from house to house, apartment to apartment, taking anything they find. If they are resisted they use superior numbers and lack of humanity as a means to an end. Women and young girls run the risk of being beaten, raped and killed.

Luckily for Bill Jones and his family, their lives are continuing. Bill saw the signs and enacted his plans prior to the curfews and martial law. Bill and the family are now living somewhat comfortably in a small doublewide trailer that Bill purchased last year. The trailer is on 15 acres of land in an unincorporated area about three hours away from their primary residence.

The Jones family has many survival advantages over their old neighbors in the city. The rural location of the PSS means that it is highly unlikely Bill's family will suffer attacks from roving gangs of marauders. If anyone does come near the PSS Bill will most likely know about it before they get there as his location provides a good view of the road leading to his property and because the road is covered in gravel Bill should hear any approaching vehicles as well.

Aside from security, Bill's family also has the ability to grow their own food in a large garden behind the PSS. Sara and Bill have both spent a great deal of time learning about gardening for food production, and now they can produce a wide variety of garden vegetables in quantities sufficient to feed their family.

Although the PSS site is not as large and comfortable as their home, it is suitable to long term living. There were many reasons that Bill and Sara chose this site and this type of structure. Let's look at Bill's planning and his Primary Shelter Site (PSS).

Evacuation

In planning his evacuation, Bill took into account the traffic patterns of the area near his home and leaving his city, as well as road conditions and alternate routes available. Bill took several opportunities to drive each of these routes at various times of the day and night to ensure he had a very good understanding of what to expect. While planning these routes Bill also made sure to notate all important locations along his routes such as gas stations, rest stops, police stations, hospitals, etc.

Bill made sure that his wife had an emergency plan in her car with routes planned from her most common locations to their primary meeting place in case they were not together when they needed to leave. Common locations for family members would include School or Work locations.

> **** NOTE ****
> Citing Operational Security, Bill has drawn the routes on the map with a special marker that will only illuminate under black light. If the family has to leave a vehicle, they don't want anyone finding it to have a map to their shelter site. Each member of Bill's family has a key chain and each key chain has a small black light attached to it in order to view the map easily.

Bill made sure his wife drove the indicated routes on multiple occasions in order to validate she was comfortable with navigating the routes without a map. Bill realized that although this was a tedious exercise, and his wife complained about it each time, the knowledge of the routes and practice driving them could be the difference between life and death for her and the children.

Bill also took several opportunities to practice loading the designated vehicle and ensuring that everything he intended to take would fit comfortably inside. This allowed him to determine a few things he would have forgotten, and to drop a few things he realized he didn't really need.

The last thing Bill verified is that each vehicle was equipped with essential emergency gear including:

- Emergency Tire Inflation Canister (x2)
- Emergency Road Flares (x6)
- Roadside Toolkit
- Emergency Flashlight with Green and Red Capabilities
- Jumper Cables
- Emergency Blanket (x4)

- Water Bottles (x12)
- Fire Extinguisher

Each family member had their BoB ready to go, so when Bill gave the word the entire family was on the road in less than 10 minutes. Due to the decision to leave the residence early in the flu event, Bill avoided having to deal with military checkpoints, traffic jams, fuel shortages and many other issues that arise during any catastrophic event. Bill also avoided becoming an obvious target by travelling while open travel was still an option and normal traffic patterns were present.

Due to the nature of the pandemic, Bill is relatively assured that he and his family will be much safer at their Primary Shelter Site (PSS) as contact with other people can be avoided. The rural location of the PSS also provides Bill and the family with additional security from random attacks or looters searching for items in the later stages of the pandemic. As well as personal freedom to move inside or outside of their PSS during day or night hours without threat of becoming a victim of the Martial Law curfews that have been enacted.

The Aftermath

It has been many years since a major flu pandemic struck humanity. No one really knows what will happen during a pandemic or how the majority of the population will react. Certainly we would like to think that people are smart and understanding and can handle a crisis of this magnitude without losing their minds. I don't believe this is the likely case.

During the 2009 Swine Flu pandemic people as a whole reacted very well and everything turned out to be okay. We were very lucky that only a few thousand people died, officially. Unofficially we can only guess at the number of deaths caused by the 2009 Swine Flu.

During the Spanish Flu pandemic of 1918 between 30 and 50 million people died, officially. This equates to roughly 2% of the global population at the time. In today's population estimates that would equal roughly 140 million dead. You must also take into account that infection will spread further and faster with modern air travel and the high number of global trekkers.

If you were watching the news during the 2009 Swine Flu pandemic and remember the fear it generated, understand that the total number of people globally that died was roughly 17,000. Try to imagine the difference if the numbers started hitting 1 million, 5 million, 25 million, 100 million. Here is a brief description of what that would possibly look like;

1) 500,000 dead – Hospitals are operating well beyond capacity. Patients are sleeping or lying dead in the waiting rooms, hallways and outside. Businesses are losing money and the stock market is plunging (if it isn't already closed down completely). Hyper-inflation has increased the prices of food and medicines to beyond the reach of normal citizens. Social services are starting to break down.

2) 1 million dead – Schools, businesses and hospitals closed. Police, Fire and Ambulances only responding to extremely important situations. Martial Law is in place with evening curfews and restricted movement throughout many cities. Food and medicine are strictly controlled. Quarantine camps will be filling quickly and becoming extremely dangerous. Military assistance with control and quarantine will be required. People currently incarcerated in prison will be either left to starve in their cells, released into the yards to fend for themselves, moved to secured quarantine zones (unlikely), or released altogether. They could potentially be looked after, but this is most likely not going to happen. USNorthCom is already activated, but now they are starting to take control.

3) 5-25 million dead – All movement is restricted. Movement without authorization may result in deadly force. Police, Fire and Ambulatory services are no longer available to regular citizens. Vast areas of major cities will be quarantine zones of complete lawlessness. Small communities will be off limits to outsiders with all major entrance points guarded. Military control via units such as USNorthCom will be complete.

4) 25+ million dead – At this point no one really knows what will happen. There are far too many people dying to bury them all. Mass burnings of bodies will create a constant black smoke and smell of death that will permeate the area for miles. Military control will break down in many areas as some soldiers decide that being with their friends and family is more important than protecting anything. There will be significant power vacuums in large cities where whoever controls the food, water or medicine will control the area. Expect criminal warlords to take full advantage of these situations.

The total aftermath of the pandemic event cannot be reliably determined until the event happens. Unlike nuclear war, terrorist attacks and other major events, this one has so many variables that it seems impossible to fathom. It can be reliably inferred that the worse the situation gets, the more casualties and problems we will see from indirect results such as crime, starvation, lack of resources, etc. This will increase the death toll as well as the difficulty in maintaining control and order.

Obviously what we are discussing here is a worst case scenario. Planning accordingly for an event of this magnitude will be very costly and most likely cause some people to think you are nuts. Make sure you say a prayer for those people after you get to your PSS.

I also believe it should be understood that although in this case the threat was from a pandemic flu, humans themselves will most likely become the largest threat to other humans. With over 7 billion people on this planet we live in a world that is barely a blink away from catastrophe. One major disruption in the massively intricate machine that is the global economy and food distribution network could not only cause harm, it could spiral the entire operation into chaos. A major flu pandemic would certainly be capable of providing this monkey wrench and setting the wheels in motion to create havoc. Once the fear begins to rise, it is only a matter of time before neighbor turns on neighbor and it's every man himself.

It should be noted that not all flu bugs are going to unleash a global pandemic. Obviously each year we all survive a multitude of bugs with very minor symptoms, even if we do whine about it. For more information about topics like pandemic flu, turn to the folks that know more than anyone else, the CDC. You can find a link to their website in Appendix B of this book.

Zombie Apocalypse

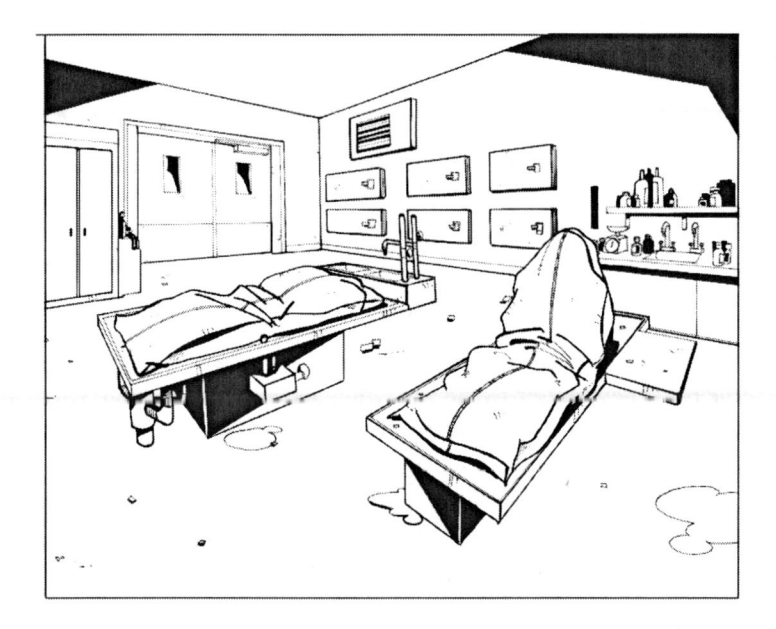

Could it happen?

Hollywood versus Reality

If you watch most of the movies and television shows regarding zombies you will notice that one thing is missing from most of them; a root cause.

You will either meet the main characters and then flash forward to the current time, which is after the zombie event, or the whole story will start after the event and you will never get more than a brief explanation for the event that caused the end of the world as we know it. One would think that something as important as the means of creation of a legion of undead or infected flesh eaters and killers would probably be at the top of the list for most authors and film producers, but it's really not.

Studios hire professionals when they make movies, and those professionals consult with the film's technical staff in order to make the film as realistic and believable as possible, well at least this is supposed to happen. When it comes to zombies though, the experts often disagree on potential causes or feel it is too difficult to explain as back story.

Some of the better zombie movies provide this backstory, which gives us the opportunity to see what kind of zombies are really out there. As far as I can tell, there are three major types of zombies.

Returned from the dead

Description - The classic zombie, this guy or gal is willing to crawl through six feet of hard packed dirt just so he or she can slowly wander the countryside searching for brains to eat. Reanimated through unknown means or possibly some form of radioactivity, these zombies weren't very threatening unless you were immobile or just plain stupid. Even though they showed great ambition in escaping their final resting spot, once free they were pretty unimpressive. Science and medicine, not to mention special effects in movies, have made leaps and bounds since this zombie ruled the screens.

Verdict – Not possible. There is nothing even remotely possible to make this happen on a mass scale. People are sometimes buried alive and come back, but those are few and far between.

Reanimation of the recently dead

Description – This zombie is one of the latest versions to hit the screens. The "recently deceased" portion of the description is the real difference maker. These people have not been buried and most likely they died at the hands of another zombie. There is still some confusion as to the nature of the reanimation, in some cases a virus is the catalyst but there are still some of this genre that use environmental causes or even things like comets passing near to the Earth.

Verdict – These zombies are good for movies, books and TV but not likely to ever come to pass in real life.

The Infected

Description – This flavor of zombie is my favorite because it has so much potential for storylines. Infection can start anywhere at any time, it can travel vast distances without notice and it has a basis in reality that humans somewhat understand. Infection can travel slowly, or it can travel quickly. It can start slow and speed up, or start fast and slow down. Infection does not require a lot of outside manipulation to create a zombie apocalypse, unlike other sources. Since the zombies are not necessarily dead, they don't need to shuffle along, they can sprint, they can think, they can even solve simple problems most likely, which makes them inherently more dangerous.

Verdict - Infection does not necessarily mean "dead" and therefore some zombie aficionados will claim this category does not fit the classic definition of ZOMBIE. I say "I DON'T CARE". Infection is by far the most likely player when it comes to a real zombie apocalypse.

Bill Takes On the Zombies

After suffering through a terrible house fire then a flash flood and finally a flu pandemic, Bill Jones thinks he's seen it all. He's moved from his PSS in rural Indiana back to his home near Chicago and has gone back to work. Luckily the flu pandemic took out his boss, so Bill got a nice promotion and pay increase just for surviving! That's just one more reason to plan and prepare!

After a while things calm down and Bill and the family get back into a normal routine. Bill still makes monthly trips out to the PSS to rotate any items that need rotating and ensure everything is in good working order. Bill has realized that preventive maintenance on things like generators, vehicles, plumbing and many other items certainly makes life a lot easier when you are trying to survive.

Most of the world has recovered nicely from the flu pandemic. It took three years to finish clearing away the bodies and ensuring that the world's population was properly inoculated against a repeat. The government of the USA decided that they would take this chance to "redevelop" some areas that weren't doing so well before the pandemic so people were relocated from the inner city area into some of the millions of empty homes left after the virus killed the owners.

With so many people being lost to the pandemic the global unemployment rate has dropped to virtually nothing. Companies are in the midst of hiring bonanzas never before seen. The usually drawn out process of submitting a resume, having a phone screen, interviewing and then going through background checks and drug screens has been virtually dropped in favor of policies to get people in the door as quickly as possible.

This lack of due diligence is now about to result in the most horrific terrorist attack ever planned or implemented in human history. In a Bio-Weapons lab deep in the hills of Virginia, a young man with an impeccable resume and educational history is carefully going through computer records in order to find a weapon to use against the "Capitalist American Regime".

On March 8th, Rahib Talur Hamadi discovered the virus he would use to send the Americans to their deaths. Utilizing his high level security access Rahib found and stole a vial of liquid labeled H1R1 Rhabdovirus "Zombie Flu".

April Fool's

March 14th, 2018. Rahib Hamadi delivered his vial of toxin to his handlers and they decided to spread the virus by intentionally infecting people in airports and subways of major cities on a specific day, April 1st.

Within 6 hours people in New York, Chicago, Miami, Los Angeles, Las Vegas and Dallas begin making their way into their local emergency rooms. Doctors initially reacted with casual disregard, not choosing to confine the sick to any form of quarantine. Over the course of the next 8 hours doctors, nurses and aides, along with the victims' families and hundreds of other patients, would make their way into and out of the emergency room areas which are now completely contaminated with H1Z1 flu.

It will not be until the victims' symptoms include bleeding from the eyes and mouth that the doctors decide to quarantine them, and by then they know they need to quarantine the entire emergency room and possibly the entire hospital.

On the 9:00pm news the local anchorman describes panic at an area hospital where the CDC has instituted a quarantine zone. Individual witnesses were calling in on telephones claiming that inside the hospital people were attacking each other and biting each other and that dozens, perhaps even hundreds were dead. Although the CDC had quarantined the hospital, they vehemently denied any such reports of violence. According to the CDC the reason for the quarantine was for containment of a virulent form of Tuberculosis. One small piece of information at the end of the segment states that there are reports from several other major cities of similar CDC activity, raising the specter of a possible flu outbreak.

Bill Jones turned off the television and went to check on his Bug Out Bag, something wasn't right about the news report. He explained his feeling to his wife and she told him she had just gotten comfortable again in their home and wasn't about to leave for the PSS again. Besides, she said, it was probably all just an elaborate April Fool's joke.

Bill thought that sounded like a pretty sick joke.

Zombie Day (Z Day)

Bill and his wife awoke to the sounds of sirens in the distance. Bill went to the window and looked outside, where everything appeared to be normal. As he turned to walk away from the window however, he caught sight of his neighbor, Jim Parker, whose wife works the night shift at a local hospital, running across the street in his bathrobe. Bill turned back to the window and watched as Jim ran full speed to the Whitehurst's house and attacked their elderly neighbor, Mr. Whitehurst, from behind as he was watering his lawn. Mr. Parker brutally hammered on the back of Mr. Whitehurst's head even after it was apparent to Bill that he could no longer be alive. Bill ran downstairs and opened his front door. Although his neighborhood appeared normal, walking into his yard and looking further down the street was an altogether different story. The view from his front yard was something he just couldn't initially believe. On the horizon he could see multiple homes on fire and cars crashed into each other as well as into homes and trees. What appeared to be people were lying on their front lawns and not moving, he didn't know if they were dead or not. He saw several people running down the street, being followed or even chased by other people.

Running back inside, Bill closed and locked the front door and picked up the phone to call 911. After multiple attempts to call 911 and receiving only a fast busy signal, Bill turned on the television just in time to hear the anchorman telling people to stay inside, lock their doors and windows and be prepared to defend themselves against attack. According to the news anchor seemingly normal people all over the city were attacking others at random.

Running back upstairs Bill tells his wife and kids that they are enacting their plans. His code for a "worst case scenario" is "Code Black" and when he tells the family this is a Code Black event, they know this is something extremely serious and that they cannot mess around or take their time getting ready to move.

Within minutes all of the family members are dressed and loading their gear into the back of the SUV as directed by Bill. Once everyone is safely loaded into the SUV, Bill takes a moment to describe what they are about to encounter. Bill explains, that due to some form of outbreak people are attacking and killing each other at random. He further explains that under no circumstances are they to roll down their windows or unlock their doors. They are to watch for anyone approaching the vehicle on their side and alert Bill if they see anyone. Bill also explained briefly that they were likely to see people dead in the streets, and potentially they may even see someone get killed, or be attacked themselves.

Bill starts the vehicle and opens the automatic garage door. The scene before him is a shock even though he has prepared for it. His neighbors are lying in the street dead while their attackers search for new prey. People wandering in the street appear confused, in shock and unable to process their surroundings. Houses are burning and cars are crashed in yards and fences.

Bill immediately decides to travel via his secondary evacuation route as his primary route takes him near a highly populated area. He drives slow enough to dodge objects in the street but too fast for a person on foot to catch the vehicle. Thirty minutes after leaving the house Bill pulls onto the highway. Traffic is backed up and people are out of their vehicles talking and attempting to find the cause of the delay. Bill immediately turns his vehicle around and heads back to the surface streets to continue his evacuation.

On multiple occasions Bill is forced to evade people in the street, both living and possibly dead. Debris is often a problem and Bill tries his best to avoid running over anything that could potentially damage his vehicle. Eventually Bill's luck runs out and he suffers a flat tire due to road debris. As rehearsed by the family on multiple occasions, Bill and Nick dismount the vehicle with their weapons and assume defensive positions around the vehicle while Bill's wife, Sara, uses the emergency tire sealant to get the tire operable again. Once completed they all return to the vehicle and resume their journey.

During his prep Bill made the decision to rent a storage site near the halfway point between his house and his PSS. By altering his route only slightly Bill is able to reach his storage site in a relatively short amount of time. There he is able to safely remove the damaged tire and replace it with a tire he has kept stores in the facility. He was also able to grab a few items that he realized he had not packed when leaving the house. In less than 10 minutes the family is back on the road and headed to their PSS site.

Bill and the family safely arrived at their PSS as the sun was setting in the west. What had started out as a day from hell had finally slowed down and seemed like a dream to Bill. As his family waited in the vehicle with the doors locked, Bill took his handgun and did a quick search of the perimeter and interior of the PSS. Once he was convinced that they were safe, he backed the vehicle up near the door and everyone unloaded their gear. Bill then parked the vehicle on the side of the trailer.

Although maintaining electricity in both locations is expensive, Bill decided it was well worth it to have access to news and weather from the PSS if it was available. Although he did not have cable television routed to the trailer, he did maintain his wireless broadband account and had ensured he had service in this location. With this ability he was able to read the local, national and international news reports online. The news was not good. According to the anchorman the virus was passed by direct contact with an infected person's bodily fluids, but the rate of infection was extremely high. Within minutes of coming into contact with an infected person the newly contaminated individual would begin to suffer debilitating headache pain, bleeding from the nose, mouth and eyes and extreme anger. CDC officials had already determined the basic elements of the virus to be Rabies, but beyond that they had not pinpointed a way to stop it. Worse news was that the virus had already mutated once, and that the entire Chicagoland area was now under quarantine, and there were already reports in 7 other major cities of possible infection outbreaks.

According to the initial reports, the infected persons are not "undead zombies" but due to the damage caused to their brain by the Rabies virus and apparent brain swelling these individuals were reduced to mere animals. As the virus progresses the swelling continues until the person ultimately dies of mass hemorrhaging.

Z Day +1

Bill sits down with the family after checking the news again. He explains that the infection has now reached all areas of the USA. When asked why the military doesn't just kill all of the infected Bill explains that many people feel the infected people still have rights, and therefore are protected against elimination. Politicians were already taking sides and making campaign promises. Aside from that the military is restricted by potential collateral damage and the pure political fear of unleashing the hell of war upon our homeland's streets.

Just as they had done before, Bill and the family set about to make their PSS a comfortable place to live. Luckily it was a good time of year for planting a small garden and the weather wasn't too bad for the region. Bill cleared the brush out of the yard between the house and the fence and took the dog for a few walks to get him used to the perimeter again.

Bill's daughter, Stephanie, cleaned the water filtration system in case they needed to use raw water. Bill's son, Nick, completed his assignments of cleaning the solar panels on the roof of the PSS and then cleared the brush from the immediate area around the trailer.. Bill completed preventive maintenance on all of the small engines and tools they would be using while his wife, Sara, did an inventory of the stockpiled goods and began cleaning the larger firearms.

After a full day of working the family settled in for a dinner of cold sandwiches and chips. They drank soda and afterwards had a snack of cookies with milk. When the pandemic struck and they had run to the PSS they had not planned for "dinner" and ended up eating MREs and canned veggies for about a week. Sara decided to fix that this time and included some food they liked when they left.

Living Apart

Living at the PSS during the Zombie Flu was not easy. Days were filled with cleaning, maintenance, gardening and other backbreaking chores. Although most of the things they did were needed, Bill was also trying hard to keep the kid's minds away from the horror the rest of the world was living through.

The most difficult aspect for Bill's children was the loss of any social contact with their peers. Over the course of the first two weeks Stephanie began dealing with the knowledge that many of her school friends were probably no longer alive. This realization led her through the thought processes regarding cousins, teachers, favorite actors and singers...all dead. The stark reality of the world she was now living in was difficult to grasp and Bill and Sara tried their hardest to help her cope with these issues.

For Nick the situation was only slightly different. Being older and more mature Nick had often discussed planning and preparing with his friends, though most of them would only laugh and poke fun at him for having a "crazy dad". Realizing that those people, his friends, would never be there to laugh with him or play video games or talk about girls had a profound affect. Nick became solemn and detached from the family.

One month after Z-Day the family gathered around the radio as Bill was finally able to locate a station that was broadcasting live. According to their reports the military had managed to clear a lot of the "zombies" from the areas near their bases and were moving into the larger cities. Progress was hampered by survivors in those areas that have taken over and established themselves as defacto leaders. The military was taking great care in trying to coax these people into cooperation as opposed to using overwhelming force to suppress them.

One week later Bill and Nick encountered their first "zombie". A young man not much older in appearance than Nick wandered into the PSS site and became entangled in a spider trap that Bill had created. The man was clearly out of his mind, as if he knew nothing other than hate and pain. Bill recognized the "symptoms" that had been reported over the radio and determined the man was infected. Without discussion he chose to protect his family and killed the infected man. That moment would haunt Bill for the rest of his life. Although he felt he was completely justified, taking another person's life even in defense of his family was not something he could easily overcome.

Surviving....Thriving

Bill and the family lived in the PSS for the next twenty four months while the infection (later referred to as H1Z1 Zombie Flu) was eradicated through a combination of military intervention and natural selection. The infected were no longer capable of logical thought and therefore were doomed from the start.

The PSS garden was able to provide the Jones family with all the vegetables they needed and they were able to add meat to their meals through hunting and trapping. When supplies of cleaners and soap ran low the family began making their own utilizing ideas Bill had learned from various survival guides.

Bill had managed to make routine runs into area communities during the outbreak where he was often able to secure small amounts of fuel and supplies. On these trips Bill always took someone with him following the "Buddy Rule". Since all members of the family were trained with the firearms it didn't matter who he took, he was still confident the PSS would remain secure.

Throughout the time at the PSS all of the family members learned a lot about themselves. Although Bill fully expected his kids to learn valuable lessons and discover self-reliance, he was shocked to find that he and Sara also went through this process. Each member of the family became a stronger version of themselves during the two years of PSS living.

After the Zombie Flu

Just over 24 months after fleeing their home in a controlled evacuation, Bill was happy to hear that people were moving back into the suburbs of the larger cities, rebuilding was beginning. The family discussed the idea of returning to the Chicago area openly and honestly. Two weeks went by and there were no further reports of zombie attacks and the military was in firm control most of the criminal elements.

Nick and Stephanie returned to the Chicago area in an attempt to reclaim their lives and assist with rebuilding operations. Both would draw upon their father's planning and preparation throughout their lives and were adamant with their own families that emergency planning and preparation were not only helpful for dealing with unforeseen circumstances, but also dealing with everyday decisions and issues. Just as Bill had learned to view life through the eye of a prepper, so too would his children. None of them were doomsayers or prophets of death and destruction, they were people that acknowledged that sometimes life throws you a serious curveball and it's better to be prepared for that pitch than it is to just swing wildly or sit back and hope that ball doesn't hit you square in the face.

Bill and Sara remained "on the farm" as they referred to it. Living the simple life suited them and being able to provide themselves with nearly everything they needed was somewhat empowering.

Bill started his own business, "Bill Jones Survival Institute" and began training people on planning and preparation procedures.

Real World Zombies

The Catalyst

The great thing about the recent Zombie phenomenon is that mainstream science is finally seriously looking into the real world possibilities of "zombies". In the past decade there have been more articles written and more thought on the subject than ever before.

One recent article suggested that a mutated form of the rabies virus coupled with a flu virus, or even weaponized, to cause moderate symptoms of encephalitis could result in an infected person suffering severe bouts of rage and becoming prone to extreme violence. Whether or not this is actually possible is not known, and it would not completely fit the criteria for "zombie", but it would certainly be well on its way. In my opinion all you need is the following:

1. Influenza – A highly virulent form of flu could be used as the carrier. This should also cause coughing and sneezing.

2. Modified Rabies virus – I don't know if you could use a flu virus to transport the rabies virus, but we are learning more about this every day. I am sure something could be engineered on a genetic level. Rabies would give our zombie a severe case of the "I hate you and want to kill you" syndrome.

3. Encephalitis – Add in something that will cause slight to moderate brain swelling under the theory that this will cause a more basal form of thought, or a more animalistic mentality for the infected person.

4. Hemorrhagic Fever – If you could manage to add in a hemorrhagic fever that would cause bleeding from the ears, eyes, nose and mouth you would have a great looking zombie.

Put all of these together and what do you get? A sick person that is extremely angry and violent for no reason. They can't communicate by words or signs, which will further aggravate them. They will be bleeding from all orifices and drooling uncontrollably. They will sneeze and cough, spraying blood, spit and virus all over anyone in the vicinity. Their lack of communication and intense anger will most likely lead them to attack people, further spreading the infection.

In its natural form rabies has a pretty long period of incubation, but this would most likely be shortened drastically if the zombie apocalypse is the intended result. In recent movies a person getting infected may go full zombie within seconds, or potentially a few hours. This makes sense based on the location and severity of the infection source. Someone bit on the hand might hold out for a while but someone with a chunk torn out of their neck is probably going to rock into zombie mode in a matter of minutes.

The Reality

When speaking of viruses carrying the necessary "zombiness" to create a Zombie Apocalypse all you have to do is look at recent discoveries in regards to gene therapy and curing sickness and disease. Several years ago there was a quite popular movie released, (based on earlier movies and a book), in which "infected" people were killing everyone on Earth and there was only one guy left in New York City. In this particular movie the apocalypse was man made by virtue of a scientific breakthrough using a virus to cure cancer. Far fetched? It certainly was five or ten years ago, but recently there was breaking news that scientists have been using HIV, the virus that causes AIDS, to cure certain diseases, and it has been successful.

The point is that we don't know what tomorrow's scientific breakthroughs are going to bring us. Rushing to cure one disease or a group of diseases may end up destroying the world a year later.

The Cure

Unfortunately for zombies and those that relish the idea of living through the zombie apocalypse, the duration of this event would most likely be extremely short. No matter the cause, there are a few things that are going to cause severe problems for the zombies.

Weather

No matter where the zombie apocalypse happens, these dudes are going to have to deal with weather. They will suffer the cold in the north, hot in the south and the moderate in between. Humidity, precipitation and wind will also have an effect.

- Heat – Zombies don't wear sunscreen and they won't change clothes if they get too hot. If they are "infected" but not "undead" then they will suffer heat stroke. If they are "undead" then their skin will shrivel up into human beef jerky and their locomotion will be severely impeded.

- Cold – Infection based zombies will suffer the same problems normal people do, mainly frostbite or hypothermia based on exposure. The "undead" zombies will freeze up and start losing parts. Cold weather would be bad for them.

- Wind, Rain, Humidity – In moderate climates the zombies will still suffer humidity, rain and wind. All of these things will take their toll and create massive difficulties for the zombie population.

Animals

After the zombie apocalypse gets started the local wildlife will most likely have something to say about it. Animals can sense that their prey is weak and they will take advantage of this. Zombies in the Bronx will need to steer clear of the Zoo, but around the globe there is likely to be some happy animals. Even the family dog may get a zombie lunch out of it. In regards to an infected zombie, whether or not this virus is communicable to the animals could change things drastically, but for all intents and purposes we'll stick with the idea that Rover is immune.

They're Clumsy Bastards

The general thought is that zombies don't tend to display much operational awareness. This means they are not really paying attention to much around them normally. This will lead to zombies falling off bridges, walking into rivers, lakes and the ocean, falling down hills and tripping over things that people leave all over the place like curbs, fire hydrants, bicycles, etc. These accidents will result in many zombies lying dead on the ground, drowned, or unable to move due to broken bones. Those that can't move can't eat. Sooner or later they'll…..die? Well, we don't know what will happen, but they will probably decompose to the point where they don't exist anymore.

The Right to Bear Arms

In regards to zombies in the good ole USofA, I don't see them lasting too terribly long. Once it is known they are dangerous and need to be destroyed by any means necessary, there will be literally millions of people running around killing them for sport or fun. Knowing our current culture it will result in at least six different reality TV shows, and probably about four million viral videos of different ways to kill a zombie. There will most likely be a disproportionately large number of husbands suffering the loss of putting down their zombie infected wives. "Your Honor, she was a zombie, I swear." I can also guarantee that some bleeding heart organization will be set up to lobby congress for Zombie Rights. Needless to say unless we run out of ammo and alcohol, the zombies won't stand a chance here.

The Military

Contrary to popular belief, the military would most likely put up a pretty good resistance to the Zombie Apocalypse. Soldiers are trained to kill and they do it well. In the movies you can only kill a zombie by destroying its brain, but in real life it is probably going to be much different.

Taking out a zombie will probably be about the same as taking out a person, perhaps even easier. Zombies are not going to utilize tactics to sneak up on you, nor are they going to put on body armor or try to use cover and concealment. When one zombie goes down, the others are not likely to attempt to help it. Lastly, the zombies aren't going to try not to get shot. When the apocalypse comes, look to the soldiers to eradicate the scourge pretty quickly.

Self-Destruction

Zombie lore always seems to include the idea that the zombies would attack living people, but not animals and not themselves. I would think the zombies would find each other quite tasty and easy to catch. For this reason I think a good number of our undead friends would probably fall victim to a hungrier version of themselves.

Natural Selection

Due to the fact that these creatures are not going to be doing anything for survival other than wandering around looking for people to eat, it is pretty easy to figure they won't last very long. Nature has a way of weeding out the less capable creatures and zombies will most certainly fall under that heading if they possess the characteristics we think they will possess. Obviously a good storyline for a novel would be zombies that can think and reason, which would lead to some great movie plots.

Survival Basics

Preparation

When discussing "Survival Basics" it must be understood that each situation will be different than the next, and planning for every eventuality is simply not possible.

For example, when preparing emergency plans Bill decided to go through a practice run with his Bug Out Bag by "roughing it" in the woods for a weekend. On the second day he was hiking to a stream and slipped on some loose dirt and leaves, badly twisting his ankle. Bill went through his bag and found that although he had a First Aid kit, it was small and did not include anything he could use to reinforce his ankle. That got him thinking; "What if I had broken my ankle? What if I had fallen into a ravine and hurt my back? What if I were attacked by a bear?....." You see where this is going?

When Bill returned home he was in a mad fury to make sure he packed for every possible emergency. Shortly thereafter he had a Bug Out Bag that he couldn't pick up and he was no longer able to pack everything into his vehicle safely. His wife found him in the garage staring at the rear of the vehicle and asked why he was upset, when he answered her by saying he was trying to pack for every possible event, she giggled in that sweet way wives often do, and then told him he was an idiot.

The point is that you CAN NOT pack or plan for every eventuality. Inevitably you will find at some point that you didn't pack or plan for something. All you can do is hope that in the process of planning and packing, you have accounted for the most likely of scenarios given your situation and geographic location. Obviously if you are in southern Florida you won't be packing arctic weather gear, and to the same point if you are in Oregon you should probably include some gloves, coats, scarves, etc …in your Bug Out Bags. Wet weather gear should be included no matter where you are located because wet generally equals cold and that usually equals uncomfortable. Use common sense and everything should be A-Ok.

Geographic Concerns

Common sense is a wonderful thing. It should be utilized immensely when completing your planning and preparing stages. If you live in an area where it gets really cold during part of the year, make sure you plan accordingly. As such, if you live in an area with little water, pack more water. If you live in an area where it is marshy and wet, pack more wet weather gear and bug repellent.

Aside from these very common concerns, there are a few things that most people don't even think about until they are told differently or find out the hard way. Here are a few things to remember about various geographic regions when making your plans:

- Cities are dangerous – Large cities are full of people that don't know how to survive without grocery stores, coffee shops and fast food delivery. Large cities also offer a lot of opportunity for ambushes and mob attacks. It is widely thought that large cities, in the worst case scenario, will turn into big war zones with the battle lines drawn between organized gangs or surviving thugs, or militarily controlled zones. Get what you need and get out fast.

- Apartments don't provide safety or security – Apartment dwellers will need to get out and find a new dwelling before things get too bad, unless they can form a strong community bond with the people in their building, and trust them implicitly. Apartments generally sport very weak barriers (doors) and walls that can be knocked through quite easily. Apartments also lack very many hiding spots or escape routes.

- Highways will be packed – If you live near a large city, don't just drive as fast as you can to the nearest highway on-ramp. Everyone knows where the highways are and they will break for them immediately. Find alternate routes that will place you on the highway a minimum of 50 miles from the nearest large city. When on the highway travel at a speed that is safe and easily controllable, but too fast for someone to overtake you easily. Be wary of other vehicles and watch the road very closely for debris or objects that appear out of place. A flat tire would be very bad in this situation.

- Weather patterns – Make sure you understand the weather patterns in your area, and the area to and at your destination. Plan accordingly and watch for changes that would indicate severe weather is approaching. Consider the annual weather patterns when choosing your PSS location and type. Example: Planning to go to your PSS in a corn field in Kansas during tornado season is probably not the best idea.

- Mountains, Lakes, Caves, Rivers, Prairies, Forests, etc – Each of these areas has their own ecosystems, challenges, benefits and drawbacks. Before you plan to escape to the mountains, you may want to go there and spend some time. If you can't stand to eat fish or are allergic to them, a lake is most likely not your optimal destination. This all falls under the common sense heading.

- Comfort versus Security – In a Worst Case Scenario event, you may end up being at your PSS for a long period of time. If your PSS is in the northern regions of the USA, it may get quite cold during the winter and you will probably need a fire to keep warm. Fire, unless carefully and correctly built, will create smoke. Smoke can be seen and smelled from quite a distance and may lead someone you don't know to your front door. You may make a new friend, or he may eat you for dinner. Roll the dice with those chances, or plan accordingly with training on fire building and disguising as well as how to stay warm without a fire. There are a lot of "comforts" out there that lead you directly down the path of limited security. How many can you think of?

Food & Water

When planning for an extended evacuation or Zombie event many people seem to follow the line of thinking..."I'll pack enough food for a few days, then plant a garden and grow my own food!". This is a fantastic idea! Now let's look at what we like to call, REALITY.

Growing Food

There are many factors involved in growing food, even in a small garden. Survival growing is difficult because most of the people trying to grow the food have never done so in their life. Most people think they'll plant some tomatoes, some corn and some beans, maybe throw some potatoes in the ground and a few weeks later they'll have a nice garden for feeding themselves and their families.

If it were this easy, no one would buy these items at grocery stores.

Here are some things to consider:

- Location – You need to know what your climate and topsoil type are good for growing.

- Capacity/Need – You need to know how much to grow without running short or wasting.

- Storage - You have to feed yourself all year, including times when growing may not be an option, like winter. (Do you know how to can vegetables properly?)

- Food Value – Grow foods that have very good nutritional value coupled with hearty growing potential. Easy to grow plus high nutrition is a definite WIN/WIN.

- Critters/Bugs – You most likely won't have pesticides handy, or know how to use them, so you need to make sure to care for your "crops" as best you can by reading up on how to protect them prior to trying to become a farmer.

- Wild Plants – Make sure to include a relatively recent copy of any book outlining edible plants in your region when packing your BoB. This will help you in the long run.

- Water – Growing plants require water. Ensure you have enough available to grow your plants without killing yourselves.

- Learn the Skill – Doing some reading and practicing in a garden at your house would probably be a tremendous boon to your survival potential.

- SEEDS – You need seeds before you can grow things.

- Toxicity – Some foods are poisonous if eaten raw but fine if cooked. Some foods are fine raw but poisonous if cooked. Some foods are even poisonous on some parts and fine on others (the green part of a tomato is poisonous).

- Mushrooms in the wild – Stay away from them. It's too hard to figure out which ones are okay and which are poisonous. Just avoid them.

Hunting and Trapping Food

Aside from growing food you will probably want to try to get some meat into your diet. For sake of argument we won't talk about raising animals for slaughter because it's a bit out of the spectrum of survival, so this means you will be hunting and trapping. We will assume for this portion of the guide that whatever event has occurred has not created a danger in eating the local wildlife. You may want to take that into consideration in the case of a real emergency though.

Hunting

Hunting can be a good source of food given that your surroundings are capable of supporting game animals and that that you are capable of killing them. Over hunting an area shouldn't be a problem if you are feeding yourself and your family. How you hunt will be determined by what you are hunting and what the local situation is in regards to alerting people to your position. As ammunition will most likely be scarce in a worst case scenario, it would be a good idea to learn to hunt with a bow if possible.

Trapping

Trapping is a great way to introduce smaller game animals into your diet without using ballistic ammunition and making lots of noise. Trapping also removes the issue of long distance tracking that is sometimes involved when hunting larger game animals. There are many types of traps and ways to deploy them. Most are relatively simple to build and set up, and almost all are easily portable. If you don't think you can handle killing animals by hand, look into traps that do the killing for you. If you are setting traps that you are only checking every few days, you may want to stick with live traps so the animal doesn't spoil before you get to it.

Successfully implementing all methods of food production and gathering can lead to a very good diet considering your circumstances. Remember to cook all meat thoroughly because these won't be farm raised cattle you are eating, these are wild animals that could be carrying sickness. Avoid at all costs the temptation of taking the easy road when you see an animal that is obviously sick, leave that one alone.

If you are in the Midwest and do a little bit of studying and practicing before the event, you could have meals on a regular basis including vegetable, fruits, meat and nuts without having to import anything from outside of the area. Studying up on plants in your region can help you add a bit of flavor and spices to your meals as well, so don't skimp out on your reading!

Before you think I forgot, yes, you can fish also. Fish offer great nutritional value and are relatively easy to prepare. I simply don't mention it in depth because considering how many people can fish while dead drunk, I figured most people wouldn't not forget when trying to survive.

Water

You need a LOT of water to survive. Water is used for hydrating your body, growing food, cleaning food, cleaning cuts and wounds, washing yourself, washing your clothes and vast other uses. If you have access to enough water, and the knowledge to utilize it, you may even be able to generate a small amount of electrical power from your water supply. This is not likely, so we won't discuss it here.

Important things to understand about water and your water supply:

- Security – Water is VITAL. In a long term survival event water will become so vital people may be willing to hurt or even kill you to obtain it. You need to know how much water you have and how long it will last.

    - If your source of water is a well or system of wells, you will need to secure those wells and keep their locations as secret as possible. Using your water as a bartering chip is possible, but you have to be able to protect it once people know you have it.

    - If your source of water is a river or stream, you need to be at the source, or as close to the source as possible, otherwise your water is not secure. Anyone between you and the source of the water can build a damn or redirect and you will lose your most precious resource.

- Purification –

    - Boiling - Boiled natural water tastes horrible. Just a fair warning. Boiling is probably the best way to clean your water supply of dangerous germs and bacteria. Anything floating on top after it boils is something you don't want to drink. Also, remember that boiled water isn't necessarily going to be clear. Get used to drinking water that doesn't look like water.

    - Purification Tablets – Purification tablets are inexpensive and readily available…for now. You will need to stock up on these for that time when boiling isn't an option.

- Filtering – Filtering water is good for getting the big stuff out. There are tons of ways to make water filters, big and small. Read up and understand the concept. Finding the proper materials shouldn't be too hard, so there's no need to pack them and carry them with you.

Health and Welfare

Your health and the health of your family should be your number one concern. In a disaster event where society as we know it is wiped out you won't be able to pop into the doctor's office for a checkup and some aspirin. Proper health will be very hard to maintain in a situation of this type, but it is imperative that the attempt be made. Undernourished or sick people are less likely to be able to work and care for themselves. Sick people require help, which causes someone else to be less able to perform their own duties, requiring more help and the hits just keep on coming after that. Lowering your immune system through malnourishment and bad health habits can lead to infection or sickness, which can be passed to other members of your family. Death comes quickly in a world devoid of major healthcare options.

Pay attention to the following:

- Hygiene – Brush your teeth, bathe, clean your hair, and wash your hands often. These things will help keep your body strong enough to fight off infections more easily. Women will still need feminine hygiene products for as long as they are available, so grab them at every chance.

- Antibiotics – If you have an opportunity to stockpile these creams, ointments or liquids, make sure you get as much as you can. Grabbing oral antibiotics won't do you much good as they have to be kept refrigerated and there is a chance of allergic reaction. Make friends with someone with medical knowledge and maybe you'll have a contact for good antibiotics when the SHTF.

- Hydrogen Peroxide – Get a bunch of it over a long period of time. I know it's harder to buy now and you can only get a limited amount per trip to the store or whatever, so stock up over time. Abrasions and minor cuts, sore throats and infected teeth or gums…this stuff helps with it all. This is a very good item for many reasons.

- Rubbing Alcohol – Everyone knows why it's important. Make sure you get some stockpiled if you have a chance.

- First Aid Kit(s) – There are a lot of good First Aid kits out there. Having one is great; having more than one is fantastic.

- Diet – No matter the situation, try to get into a somewhat healthy diet. There is no use in going through the pain of surviving just so you can die of diet related causes later.

- Vitamins – This goes into the "DIET" category, but I wanted to break it out on its own for emphasis. Vitamins are good for you to have. Make sure you have them.

- Toilet Paper – Amazingly, most people forget this very basic item.

In a worst case scenario where the social fabric of our society unravels and we are thrust into a post-apocalyptic setting these health and hygiene tips will not only make you easier to tolerate, but they can also save your life. Without antibiotics or many medicines even a simple cut on the hand or ingrown toenail could mean a long and painful spiral into loss of a limb or even death.

Having available medicine will also place you in serious danger if other supplies are running out. If you don't understand why having medicine might be dangerous, imagine what you would do to get medicine if a loved one was dying. Keep your medicine stash under tight lock and key and try not to let anyone know about it unless you are part of a community that requires sharing all resources. If you are in one of these you will need to decide for yourself what you share and what you hide.

Weapons / Protection

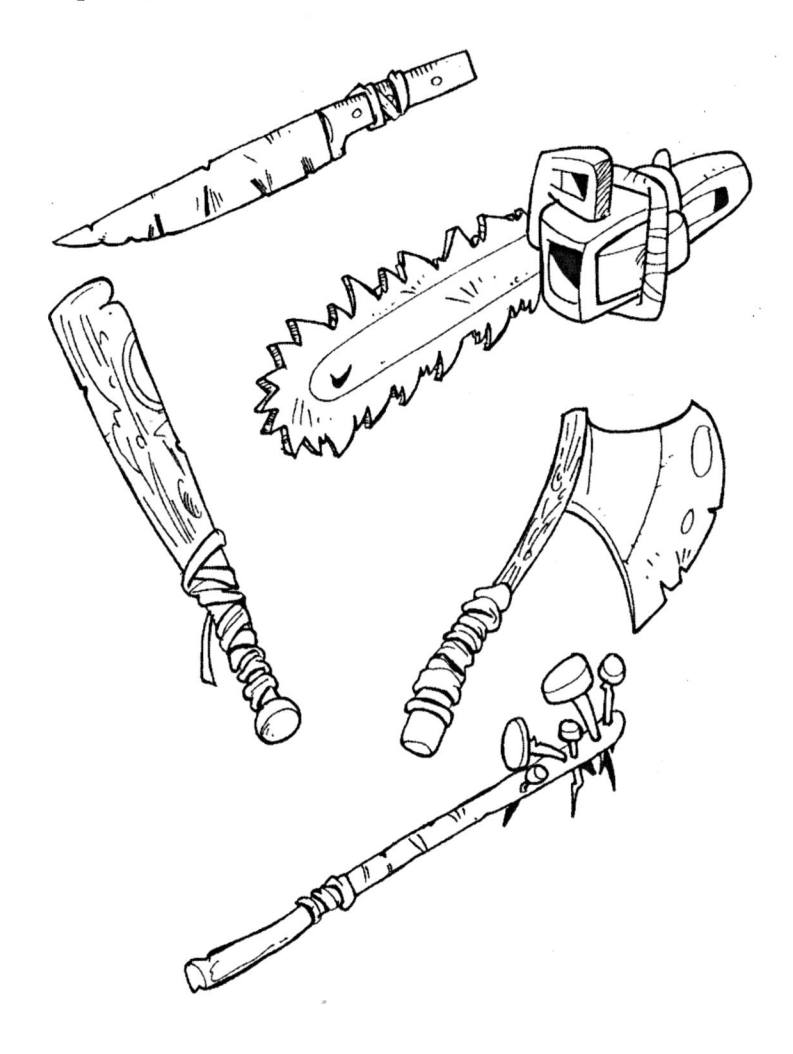

This is a touchy subject for a lot of people when they first start trying to prepare for emergencies and disasters. Each person has their own opinion in regards to the necessity of items of this sort, and these opinions are generally pretty strong. I have not met very many people that when asked whether or not they would own a gun they say "Eh, doesn't matter to me!"

I find that one of the easiest ways to approach this decision is by weighing the needs with the pros and cons. Determining the weight of each is your personal matter to contend with.

Need (Uses):
- Edged Weapons (Knife, Axe, Machete, etc)
    - Used for skinning animals
    - Used for opening items (cans, etc)
    - Used for cutting items (rope, cloth, etc)
    - Used for gathering wood (chopping, cutting)
    - Used for clearing brush or overgrowth
    - Many other common uses
- Ballistic Weapons (Bow/Arrow, Crossbow, Gun)
    - Used for hunting
    - Used for protection against animals
    - Used for protection against aggressors
    - Used for signaling

Pros:
- Very useful
- Offer a degree of protection
- Offer a degree of intimidation

Cons:
- Dangerous

Many people agree that a weapon (we'll assume "GUN" here) in the hands of a trained individual with decent morals and ethics is a valuable and important tool. Suffice it to say proper safety precautions should be followed, but that is the same with dangerous items like tent pegs, potato peelers, nail files and rubbing alcohol.

When considering firearms in your kit, please make sure that you address the following concerns:

- Training – Everyone in your group capable of firing the weapon should be trained in safely utilizing it, or trained to specifically never touch it. This should be done PRIOR to the event occurrence.

- Ammunition – If your scenario plays out for an extended period of time you may not have enough ammunition to last the duration. Correcting this issue after the fact is generally accomplished through scavenging. If possible you might want to take some time to learn how to reload your own rounds, and plan accordingly to stockpile enough materials to complete a few rounds of reloads.

- Care and Maintenance – Knowing how to fire the weapon safely is a good start, but if you don't know how to properly care for the firearm and maintain it, you won't have it for long. Most modern firearms don't stand up to the elements very well without continuous cleaning and oiling. Mr. Murphy will tell you that it will misfire when you need it to work the most.

- Limit your Calibers/Gauges – If you carry six different weapons that fire six different types or sizes of bullets you are causing yourself a lot more grief than is necessary. Plan accordingly and try to limit your weapons to specific gauges and calibers to allow bullets to be used in multiple weapons. Also try to use commonly utilized weapons platforms (calibers and gauges) as you are much more likely to be able to scavenge parts and ammunition for them.

Stockpiling

This section is simply to explain the difference between "packing" and "stockpiling".

Packing is done at your permanent residence and involves gathering the things you need to get to where you are going.

Stockpiling is the gathering of large amounts of items at your permanent residence or your PSS in the hopes that you never need them.

Stockpiling is hard to do, because it costs money to buy things that aren't at your normal location for you to use. These items sit in storage, where hopefully they are safe and secure. If you never use them, the money can either be considered "wasted" or "well spent" according to your opinions.

In regards to your stockpile area you will find some items require certain atmospheric conditions to stay fresh or usable for long periods of time. Instead of trying to match all of those criteria, I offer the following suggestions.

- Dry – Keep your stockpile area dry and non-humid if possible

- Cool – If you can keep the area below 60 degrees Fahrenheit most of your stocks should keep longer

- Darkened, but not black – There are many who contend that light speeds the processes involved in spoiling. I don't know if this is true, but why take the risk. You don't want the area pitch black though as many molds and fungi apparently like that type of setting. Also, you don't want to waste artificial light just to peruse your goods.

- Secure – Make sure your stockpile location is secured properly. It should be the most difficult place to access in your PSS.

Stockpiling Food

Contrary to popular belief just because something is in a can doesn't mean it can be stored for 10 years and never spoil. When you are planning your stockpile you have to look at the dietary needs of your family or community unit and determine what will be needed to keep them not just stay alive, but healthy and somewhat happy.

As you begin your stockpiling you will need to create and maintain very good records of what you are placing in your stockpile, when you are placing it there and when it needs to be rotated out due to expiration. One of the best ways to ensure proper rotation at your permanent location is to add your items into your normal cooking rotation. In this type of setup you actually move items from your stockpile into your kitchen or pantry for planned meals, and as you shop, you replace those items in your stockpile. This is a 3 way rotation as you have 1) Kitchen food 2) Stockpile Food Ready (this is next in line to use) and 3) Stockpile Food Reserve (this food will replace the Stockpile Food Ready supply as it is used.

In order to properly organize this craziness you can either creatively design your own methods, or if you desire there are ready made solutions available, some of which are very nice. Some simple ways to start your organization include using a permanent marker to begin marking items with the date when you buy them. Mark all items you already bought with a large "UN" for "Use Next" instead of trying to remember when you bought them. Trying to decipher the actual perishable date is not always easy, so use general guidelines for the type of food and how it is packaged and move forward from the date of purchase. Err on the side of caution for rotating out of stock though.

Something most people don't think too much about is whether or not the family will actually eat the food you are stockpiling. Remember to stockpile what you already eat, don't use the end of the world as a method for starting a new diet. Obviously you won't (or shouldn't) be stockpiling frozen pizzas and ice cream, but don't stockpile a ton of something that no one is going to eat unless you plan on trading it at some point, and even then you take a risk that is will actually be worth something.

For those people that are already living the dream, and by that I mean you live in a safe and secure location where you are already actively growing your own food potentially raising livestock and laying birds, stockpiling foods might not be your biggest concern. If you feel that the world is due for a financial collapse or that the power grid is going to fail you are already in good shape and can use your stockpiling abilities for a different purpose: Trade

Stockpiling Trade Goods

If stockpiling food is not a huge concern for you then you should consider stockpiling trade goods. Some of the more common goods that will be valuable for trade that you could stockpile are:

- Spices
  - Sugar
  - Salt
  - Pepper
- Honey
- Coffee
- Chocolate
- Alcohol

Spices will be important in trading because they will be extremely hard to get. Most people would think that living without those luxuries wouldn't be difficult, and they are right, but imagine what you would give to enjoy them every now and then after you hadn't for a long time. The difficult thing about spices is determining trade value and packaging the item in small quantities. You won't be running to the store for plastic containers.

Honey should retain a high value. Its uses are incalculable and it never goes bad. Honey can be used to lure animals for trapping, sweeten foods and drinks, treat sore throats and minor wounds, remove parasites, soften skin and many other things. Aside from stockpiling honey you may even want to consider keeping beehives and becoming a producer.

Chocolate is going to become scarce after the end of the world, no matter the cause. I would not spend a lot of space, money or time stockpiling tons of candy bars, but having a few pounds of DARK chocolate kept in an area 60-70 degrees in temperature might not be a bad idea. Dark chocolate can last probably close to 10 years, but don't try storing milk chocolate; it will go bad in only a few months.

Alcohol in the form of Whiskey, Bourbon, Vodka, etc will retain high value. Just like honey it has many different potential uses and it will become somewhat difficult to find after the SHTF. However, alcohol can be manufactured using techniques not too difficult to master. If you have the ability, time and available space you could consider growing the materials and brewing your own beer, as this would most likely have an extremely high value if it were palatable.

Primary Shelter Site (PSS)

What is a PSS?

The Primary Shelter Site is the evacuation destination that you would most likely travel to in case of an emergency. Most of your evacuation planning should be done to reach this location as quickly and efficiently as possible. This should be a standing structure if possible, meaning that your shelter is permanent and securable. This location should be able to provide you with permanent shelter in the case that your primary residence becomes uninhabitable or unreachable. Let's list a few things about the PSS. (the below list is not in order of importance)

    1) Capable of year round shelter
    2) Defensible
    3) Capable of small/medium garden growth
    4) Near a fresh water source
    5) Private/Secluded but not remote

There are many more things that you certainly should hope for in a PSS, but these are the initial characteristics we want. The requirements of your PSS change with any change to your situation or status, as well as changes in the surrounding world.

In regards to fresh water for your PSS, the ideal situation would be a natural well on the property that can be secured and controlled. Freshwater springs and streams are nice, but unless you are near the source, you cannot control the water. In extreme survival situations water could become extremely scarce and valuable. You must always remember that you MUST have water to drink.

Privacy and seclusion will be important to your safety and security initially. In the case of a pandemic you will want to eliminate or control any contact with outsiders. This will need to be tempered with the idea that once the epidemic is passed you may need to remain in your PSS for a while longer. If this is the case, having connections and access to a local community would be a good idea.

Choosing your PSS Site

Once you have narrowed down the region you would like to have your PSS located in, you will need to find the proper site. Site selection can be the determining factor in whether you survive, thrive or die. Let's look at some of the contributing factors for selecting your PSS Site.

- Access to fresh water – This should be a no brainer

- Access to woods/forest – A small wood or forest can provide materials, food, game and many other essentials.

- Defensibility – Try to imagine securing the location and defending it. If you can think of easy ways to get in, so can other people.

- Top Soil – You will probably need to grow some food, make sure you aren't on clay, rock or some other ground type not conducive to growing plants.

- Climate/Weather patterns – Ensure you are well prepared for the normal seasonal changes and that your location isn't on a flood plain or a washout area. Make sure you aren't in an area known for being unreachable in winter time due to snowfall, avalanche, etc.

- Local Building Restrictions – Ensure you know the local building regulations because securing your PSS may require some building work to be done. Waiting on permits and approvals can get harrowing.

- No City Water – Do not purchase property for your PSS that is on City Water without a natural well as backup. In a worst case scenario your city water will most likely fail as the local municipality running it fails. City water supplies are also targets for attack and targets for scavengers.

- Septic versus City – I prefer septic if you can get it cleaned out each year and keep it in good working order without maintenance. Suffice it to say in a worst case scenario a compost toilet may be your best bet if you can handle it.

Building your PSS

If you have the financial means to build your PSS from the ground up you will certainly have many options to choose from in regards to security, safety, manageability, etc. Most people will not have this option, but we will discuss it for those that can manage it.

Whether you decide to build a normal "weekend getaway" home and stock up when the shit hits the fan, or you are in open talks with companies that make hardened shelters, settling on the type of PSS you need is a decision unique to each individual. Finances will generally drive the decision into a general category and then personal opinion will continue from there.

Hardened shelters are expensive. Hardened shelters are also problematic because most of them are underground, which means if there is a structural fault you might not get out, ever. Another disadvantage of the underground shelter is that once the people you are hiding from know it's there, either they have to go away, or you have to go away. Generally speaking underground shelters have one way in and one way out. All the bad guy has to do is sit and wait for you to come out. If he finds a way to disable your fresh air intake (if there is one), then he can hasten the time that you come out. The chances of this happening are slim, but then again, you are planning for an event that has a slim chance of occurring also. Roll the dice.

You can also harden shelters that are above ground. Obviously they will not be AS secure as the underground variety, but they aren't nearly as expensive and if you are under siege by bad guys you have a much better chance of slipping away. The options for these structures are endless. Ballistic glass, reinforced concrete, closed air systems with CO_2 scrubbers and oxygen generators, hydroponic plant growing systems, water filtration systems, solar and wind power....the list goes on and on.

If you have enough money you can live out the apocalypse in relative comfort and ease. If you are broke, like most of us are, you can still survive you just won't be playing video games while you do it.

Securing your PSS

One of the first things you will want to concentrate on when facing a major event is the security of your immediate surroundings. Security can mean lots of different things based on lots of different factors. We can discuss a few of them, but for in-depth discussions of security you will need to seek information elsewhere as it is too large of a scope for this book.

As I said, security can mean a lot of different things. If you are holed up in your home in a populated area, your security perimeter will generally refer to your doors, windows and walls. If you have a fenced in yard you could possibly extend your perimeter to the fence if you have the available materials and manpower. In the case of a populated area you will find that, generally speaking, the larger your perimeter the more materials and manpower it will take to secure it. In a rural environment, the lack of a fence or natural perimeter such as a forest or tree line can in and of itself provide a buffer zone perimeter. This would be a soft perimeter requiring no extra materials, but also providing no resistance without your direct intervention.

Security can also include obstacles, traps, warning devices and patrols with people or animals or both. A good method for securing your perimeter is to set audible or visual warning devices outside of your physical perimeter, ensuring your physical perimeter is secure with patrols and physical checks and also utilizing autonomous sentries (aka dogs) to warn you of potential breaches at the perimeter. I understand this is nothing new, but some people need the advice.

Obstacles outside of your perimeter should not be large things that must be climbed over or around, as they will also block your sightlines and limit your visibility. External obstacles if employed should be trenches, holes, tripping hazards and other low lying obstacles that make traversing the environment difficult. Take into account that if you need to escape through these obstacles you will need a clear path to do so quickly and effectively, so plan accordingly.

Obstacles serve a very narrow focus and should only be utilized if you know you are going to be getting unwanted visitors attempting to breach your perimeter. Generally speaking a perimeter barricade coupled with some large and loud dogs will dissuade most people from attempting to get any closer.

Many people will instruct you to create multiple levels of security, meaning multiple perimeter barricades. This requires vast amounts of resources and much more overhead to ensure that breaches do not or have not occurred. In some cases multiple perimeters can also create areas in your perimeter that are easier to breach than a single barrier system due to visibility.

Resist the temptation to add sharp objects to your perimeter. Many people will suggest barbed wire and/or sharpened spikes on perimeter barricades, but in the event that your position is being over taken you may need to beat a hasty retreat without having access to a designated egress point. It sure would suck to have to go through the barbed wire and spikes to get out. If you really want to add these extra deterrents to your perimeter, then you need to make sure you create at least one if not two rapid egress points. This can be done by creating a designated spot where removal of the deterrents is set up specifically to be quick and quiet. Don't trap yourself.

Operational Security (Op Sec)

Operational Security is an extremely important subject when preparing for potential disasters. The range and depth of this subject is astounding and trying to convey all aspects of it in this book is impossible. True Operational Security would have to be considered in all phases and at all times during preparation, initiation and during the aftermath of a disaster. There is NEVER a good time to relax on Op Sec. Although this subject could easily fill an entire book on its own, here are some brief highlights.

During Prep

During your preparations keep in mind that anything your neighbors know you have, they will remember when the time comes that they need it. To curb this from becoming a major problem, ensure to follow the guidelines below:

- Try to bring in supplies in small, unnoticeable amounts on a regular basis.
- When bringing in large amounts of items, attempt to do so from the seclusion of a garage, or at night when neighbors are less likely to know see what you have.
- When practicing your Bug Out routine, try to do so at night or in the privacy of your garage.
- Do not speak openly to your neighbors about your plans unless you are planning to involve them and have a high level of trust in their discretion.
- If you purchase land and a PSS home, make sure that when stocking the home or preparing the area around it that any neighbors in that area are unaware of your activities.
- For your PSS, especially if you are not there often, invest in an automated alarm system. The cost per month will surely be offset by the peace of mind that you have protection for everything you are storing there.
- Keep all items, both at your home and your PSS out of the direct line of sight from anyone in your yard, or even in your home. Try to find a spot where no one should be going or looking for storage of these items.
- Ensure that all members of your family or group are well versed in any and all weapons that you have available (cleaning, maintaining, safety and use).

During Bug Out

While in the process of Bugging Out your Operational Security is paramount. If you are actively evacuating, that means other people will probably either already be doing the same thing or will be told to do so shortly. The Bugging Out process is the most dangerous of any because you are outside of your security zones (Home and PSS). Things to consider while in the process of evacuating:

- Anyone that approaches your vehicle should be considered a potential threat. Obviously how you meet that threat will change depending on whether you know the person or not, but remain cautious and ready even if it is your neighbor of 15 years.

- Maintain a safe following distance when driving and be prepared to use the left and right lanes to escape any dangers that present themselves.

- If possible, slow your vehicle at yellow and red lights but attempt to keep rolling until the light turns green. It is easier to start from a roll than to start from a stop.

- Watch for multiple vehicles that appear to be operating in chorus. This could be a potential rolling roadblock heading your direction.

- Watch for any road debris or obstacles on or near the road. The goal is to reach your destination without stopping if possible. A stopped vehicle is an easy target, and objects on or near the road can hide items meant to disable your vehicle or people waiting to ambush your vehicle.

- If you see a barricade or roadblock ahead, and it is obviously not being run by the local police, attempt to turn around and find an alternate route. Do not roll up and stop, bad guys can barricade a road too.

- Avoid obvious choke points or routes that provide good cover near the road, these are good ambush sites.

- Ensure that any children in your vehicle are not offering themselves as easy targets in their windows. Ensure that all windows are rolled up at all times and doors remain locked.

- As you near your PSS location, be wary of any vehicles that appear to be behind you or following you. It would be best not to approach your PSS until you are confident that no one is tailing your vehicle.

- Be vigilant in your awareness of your surroundings and weather conditions. Maintain the ability to adapt fluidly to changing situations and conditions.

At Your PSS

Once you have arrived at your PSS location there will most likely be a temptation to immediately roll out of the vehicle and start unpacking, this should be avoided. If you have opted for perimeter security and can say with a high degree of certainty that your perimeter has not been breached, then I would suggest entering your secured area and proceeding with a sweep of the area. If you have opted for a guard or attack dog, now would be a good time to let the animal make a run around the location.

Once you are relatively secure in the knowledge that your site is not breached and you were not followed, you can unload your vehicle and begin unpacking your site. During this process maintain a high level of readiness so you are not surprised by an intruder.

After clearing the vehicle and getting all of your gear secured in the PSS it would be a good idea to make a more thorough sweep of the area to ensure that no one has been there and left in the recent past. The goal is to know with a high degree of certainty that your location is not known by people that might decide to come back while you are sleeping. Once the sweep is done, you have completed the Bug Out process and can now relax….a little.

Once you are dug into your PSS, Operational Security still remains a top concern. I cannot however go into many more details as each person's needs will be different based on their setup, needs and situation. Some main points that will ring universal however are as follows:

- If you set up regular security patrols, ensure that the times and routes are varied so you don't accidentally start following a predictable pattern. Once you have a pattern developed, your security is severely flawed.

- If you set up regular foraging excursions, ensure that the times and routes are varied, and do NOT travel the same places enough to leave obvious trails. Beaten down grass, paths worn in dirt and weeds that have a clear route through them will lead straight back to you, and anyone that can see can follow them.

- If you utilize a tool that creates a loud or rhythmic noise, try to use it over a broad period of time and try to break your impacts up into irregular intervals. Anything that can be recognized as a pattern will be attributed to people, and therefore could easily draw a crowd.

- Try to recognize the dangers of comforts like fire, or smoking a cigarette. At night these things can be seen from great distances, (even a single cigarette can be seen from a mile away on a pitch black night). Aside from the sight of the fire or cigarette, the smalls generated by these things can be detected for several miles, and easily followed.

- Over time at your PSS you will generate trash and waste. Trash should be stored securely and not allowed to just blow away in the wind. A good tracker will notice that trash quickly. Human waste (if indoor plumbing is not available) should be handled with great care. Study concepts for waste management in the wild to avoid placing your family in danger by improperly disposing of these waste products.

How do I....?

The most difficult thing about planning for an event like a zombie apocalypse is that you don't know what you are going to need to know to survive and thrive. Amazingly in movies and books most of the things you need to know are either figured out on the run or an expert in the field is located and brought into the fold almost magically. In the real world you would have multiple people standing around scratching their heads and saying things like "I wish I knew..." and "Never thought I'd have to do this...". So, in response to that reality I am putting down a list of things you need to try to learn prior to the Zombie Apocalypse. This is not a complete list and some things on it you might not find useful in your opinion. I tend to err on the side of caution. These are **NOT** listed in order of importance.

1. Basic to Intermediate Gardening / Growing for Food – Kind of obvious why this is important

2. Food storage and packing techniques – Again, pretty obvious subject matter

3. Basic Butchering Techniques – Food related again

4. Basic survival skills – Definitely something you want to have

5. Basic plumbing, electrical, carpentry skills – If you have the luxury of needing these, you will wish you had them

6. CPR – This is something everyone should have

7. Basic Firearms skills – If you are going to be around them, learn to use them properly

8. Basic land navigation skills – Learn to use a compass and read a map, preferably a topographical map

9. Basic First Aid – A must for anyone

10. Advanced First Aid – A good thing to have

11. Basic Water Purification – A must

Again, that list is not complete, as there are always things you should know that you don't. I have also compiled a list of things that you might want to check into before the event. If you really want to know, this is my list that I have compiled for myself, in addition to what is above.

1. Basic small engine repair and maintenance

2. Basics and Advanced solar power solutions

3. Basics and Advanced wind power solutions

4. Basic motors and turbines

5. Basic and Advanced hunting techniques

6. Basic and Intermediate Hand to Hand combat techniques – Martial arts training could be very useful

7. Basic Takedown and Control techniques – Important to know what to do once you have them there

Once again this is a short list of things that I feel are important to have knowledge at the ready. You never know if you are going to need this knowledge until it's time to use it, and if it isn't available, you are pretty much screwed. If your PSS is a permanent structure it would be a good idea to purchase books on the above mentioned subjects as reference material. Obviously books are a poor resource for certain skills and knowledge, but they will still provide more information than you had prior to reading them on most accounts.

The Event

Moving to your PSS

Moving from your primary residence to your PSS will most likely be the most dangerous time after the initial event. This is obviously determined by the event itself, but in most cases if you are alive and capable of movement, this is when things will get hairy.

Some events will have a brief period of buildup in which movement will be relatively easy, such as before a hurricane, or when flu has yet to become a pandemic. Deciding to leave for your PSS at this time may seem like over reacting and if the threat never materializes it may well be, but moving at this time also may save your life and the lives of your family members.

Events such as terrorist attacks, bomb detonations, volcanic eruptions, earthquakes and many others are not generally precipitated by a warning or buildup. Fleeing after these events will place you in the same boat as nearly everyone else in the region, so having a solid plan and having the right tools will give you the edge you need to survive. Be wary, this also makes you a very good target.

Get to your PSS as quickly and safely as possible. The more chances you take with your luck, the more likely you are to run out at a very inopportune moment.

Mob Rules

Unprepared people will react in many ways. In the beginning most people will be in shock, unable to make the necessary moves to ensure their safety. A relative few people will adjust to the situation and prepare on the run. Some of them will survive, some won't. If they are lucky to get in with a group of likeminded individuals, they will have much better chances.

A small group of people will turn to crime. This will vary from theft of items to assault, rape and even murder. These individuals may also band together to form large groups intent on taking what they want or need from anyone that crosses their path. Initially these groups will function in larger metropolitan areas but once things calm down they will venture out along highways and most likely even into suburbs of large cities.

The most likely result of this gang activity will be limited to the remains of large cities and their surrounding areas but even rural areas could see the rise of localized groups of thugs bent on controlling movement and trade. This isn't a movie and the thugs most likely won't have a soft heart under their hostile demeanor. Steer clear unless otherwise impossible.

The Price of Tea In China

One thing most people fail to understand is the likely economy of a post-apocalyptic or societal crash event. When something of this magnitude happens and banks go offline money will take on a whole new meaning. Depending on the type of event that occurs, one of two things will happen to your paper and plastic money;

> 1) Devaluation – This means your paper money and credit cards aren't worth anything. People are trading in metals, guns, ammunition, food, medicine, etc. Some people may take watches or other items of intrinsic value.
>
> 2) Hyperinflation – This would be less likely after a critical event as this alludes to the idea that globally things are still running okay. If that is the case however, this would be the loss of value of the US Dollar while foreign currencies retain their value. A loaf of bread that yesterday cost you $1.99 may now cost you $300, while if you paid in Euros it would still cost the same both days.

During the event people that did not plan or prepare will likely be handing over everything they have to get simple items like guns, ammunition, food and medicine. Traders will take everything they feel will have value in the future, or things that have value now and may once again. Not all traders are savvy in this regard so trading your $2000 watch for a nice gun and some ammo would probably be a good idea if he'll go for it. In the long run the safety of you and your family is much more important than the bits of gold, silver and platinum you are wearing on your body.

After the event has occurred and things have settled down, prices will level out and a baseline will be found. Contrary to popular belief, stocking up on gold is not a good idea. No one has traded in gold in a long time, so not many people know how to trade in gold, nor will they know how to value it. Currently gold is tied to the US Dollar, so there is not an easy way to revalue it if the dollar fails. Lower value metals like silver, copper, tin and aluminum may take on value for trade. Most likely trade prices will be rather arbitrary for a while. Here are some examples of items that will have trade value;

- Guns and Ammo – Guns will retain a high trade value, as will ammunition.

- Alcohol – Whiskey, Vodka, Bourbon etc. All will retain some value.

- Medicine – High value.

- Water – High/Strong value.

- Food – High/Strong value.

- Fuel/Gas – High/Strong value.

- Sex – Women will most likely still have the ability to get goods/services for trade.

These are all just basics. Many things will have value depending on your geographic location and the needs of the people and communities in the area. Being part of a community can also lower prices as you can barter with increased buying power, assist with security in the general area around your community, offer lodging or food and many other things that individuals cannot provide.

Always keep in mind that value is relative. If you have tons of fuel, the value of that fuel to you is lower than it is to someone that has none. If you need medicine, a community with two large hospitals and a clinic may have medicine for a much lower price than a community with only a small pharmacy. If you rely on an independent trader, he will certainly be looking for a cut in the action. If you develop your own trading partners and routes, you can get more for less usually.

Aftermath

Community Rules

In the immediate aftermath of a worst case scenario event most people will retreat into their own personal spaces and protect themselves and their loved ones. Once the immediate threat is passed and people begin to venture out they will more than likely start looking at forming up the community bonds again. Depending upon the type and severity of the event, community may be the best way to go if you can get into one that is run properly. Unfortunately, properly running a community may not be what you think.

- The Right to Bear Arms – Some communities may decide to confiscate all weapons from people living in the community in order to ensure no one inside the community attempts to forcibly take supplies or materials. Securing the weapons also ensures that local law enforcement is better armed than those they enforce the law upon. Forget protesting for your 2nd Amendment Rights, the rule of law has changed now.

- Socialist Pigs – Communities surviving on their own will most likely turn to socialism. Every resource within the community will belong to the community. Individual ownership will no longer matter in regards to supplies, materials, medicines, food, etc. Before you go complaining just remember, you may need something you don't have, and then you'll be thankful the owner can't say no.

- Hard Work Sucks – In a community setting everyone will have a job to do. Most likely even the kids will have some sort of community responsibilities. Unfortunately for those of us without advanced skill sets we will be relegated to manual labor. No sick days, no vacation days. The community requires service from you and if you don't provide the service, you may not be long for the community. Also, if they make you leave they most likely won't let you take much with you.

- Draft Dodgers – Communities will require people to protect them. If there are not enough people willing to do so voluntarily, people may be forced into service. Perhaps it will be a choice between service in the guard or life outside the wire, the decisions can be tough.

- Church/Governance – The backbone of many rural communities is the local church. It would be logical that in the event of a major disaster the church would once again rise to become not only the place for local worship, but also the local seat of government. Attendance may be mandatory in order to ensure community solidarity.

- The Word of Law – Not a fan of the current prison system? Think courts are too soft? Too harsh? Well, it's a brave new world now. Criminals in the new communities will most likely be dealt with swiftly and economically. Most serious crimes will result either in banishment from the community or death, and death will come quick. Small crimes like drunk and disorderly will probably result in a whack on the head and a night in the jail, but just about everything else worth dealing with is going to fall under the "serious crime" heading. Communities don't have the resources or the inclination to deal with troublemakers, look for the gallows to make a comeback because bullets are too important.

So basically if you don't mind hard work, sharing, abiding by the law, going to church and doing your part to secure your community, then you might just fit in really well in a properly managed community.

Unfortunately due to human nature, there will be a scarce number of properly run communities. Most communities will be run by a single individual that had the upper hand over the local population when the event occurred. This person either finds himself in a position to take control because he has goods, services, money and trade items or he was already in a position of control politically when the shit hit the fan. These types of communities will quickly devolve into black holes that suck up resources from everyone around them for the good of a few. Look for brothels and saloons to be the mainstay in these towns. Forced servitude makes a comeback under management of this type. Escape as soon as you see the signs, or force a change through any means necessary.

Building Your Community

Most communities will rise from the ashes of existing communities. Existing communities provide many advantages such as constructed buildings, available goods and services, infrastructure and a sense of normalcy. If the majority of the people in the community are from the original community then there is another advantage as they already know, and hopefully trust, the others in town.

If you live in a community of this sort, making drastic changes to the physical layout of the area will not be efficient. Farms will most likely be outside of the community while shops and municipal buildings will be in the town center. Care will need to be taken to secure the routes from the local farms to the interior of the community as quickly as possible to ensure that all food grown for the community makes it into the community. Small gardens can be built within the town limits.

If the town supported a population of 5000 people before the event, but there are now only 500 people left, consider removing unused homes and businesses and utilizing the building materials and anything found inside as best you can for other projects such as barrier fences, watch towers, etc. Areas cleared of buildings can become areas to grow food thus creating a more secure environment for the community.

If you are planning your community from scratch a strong approach is the "Wagon Wheel and Spoke" system. This system is a large circular layout with a circular growing area in the center divided further into wedges for different crop rotation strategies. Approximately ¾ of the distance from the center of the circle to the perimeter will be a concentric ring designated for housing and business needs. The outer perimeter of the structure is a small buffer zone between the community and the external walls or barricade as well as light manufacturing. This structure allows for food stores to be secured and easily transportable, it also allows the field workers to work in a secure environment.

These large circular cities should have a diameter of approximately ½ to ¾ of a mile to encompass a large enough area to house the citizens as well as the crops. Obviously in many regions of the country this is not possible, so adaptations to this plan would be necessary. Security barriers and walls should be built over time utilizing watch towers in the interim between construction start and completion. As growth proceeds, additional communities can be built adjacent to the original

A city of this size should accommodate a good number of people. Although many people follow the old adage that you need one square mile of land area to support each person in a "hunter/gather" situation, this is non-sense. My reasoning on this is that although not everyone knows how to grow crops, in a community you will most likely have at least one if not several people that do have this knowledge, or at least a base understanding. Through the process of teaching others you can multiply that knowledge relatively quickly and manage larger numbers of people in a small land area. Even in a post-apocalyptic situation it is doubtful that humans will regress to a strictly hunter/gatherer existence. People that would fall this far will certainly opt for looter/scavenger before hunting and gathering, and you will likely not see this on a community scale as those people will form much smaller bands or run as individuals.

One drawback of this system is the central placement of the crops. In the case of a fire in this area some crops will ignite easily and burn fast. One counter to that problem would be a centrally installed water source and pumping system that can reach all areas of the crop section. Equally spaced water pumping stations should be placed in the secondary ring as well to counter any accidental or malicious fire in that ring as well.

One option to the "Wagon Wheel and Spoke" is to remove the interior crop section and place the crops in the areas surrounding the community. Although this lowers the security level of the food source, it requires much less space for the inhabitants to build barriers and walls around. In this situation the community would need a stockpile location that can be easily secured within the city to store large amounts of food products in case of an attack, natural disaster, etc.

Another option would be a combination of the two systems mentioned already. In this scenario the majority of the crops would be grown outside of the city walls while specific crops are grown inside. The interior crops should be chosen based on either their value or their ability to grow in small spaces. Examples would be tomatoes, potatoes, string beans, etc.

Over time wooden barricades and walls could be replaced with stronger and more secure substances such as concrete. Changes such as this would be quite permanent and should only be undertaken after the city has reached its full potential in size and scope.

Concerns such as the threat of fire and durability will also assist in the decision to move forward with a more permanent solution. These cities will evolve over time, possibly taking years to move from their humble beginnings to a more robust and self-sustaining town.

Once permanent barriers are in place (concrete walls and watch towers) the internal buildings will also most likely receive a makeover to become more durable and larger. At this time adjoining communities should be launched in order to provide space and resources for a growing population.

Major Events That Require Preparation

Throughout history things have occurred that caught people off guard. Disasters have occurred that left thousands of people with nowhere to go, nothing to eat and no water to drink. In the time since the advent of television and especially video cameras we have seen how people in the city react to these events: Rioting, Looting, Murder, Rape and Theft.

In the aftermath of Hurricane Katrina there were videos all over the news showing people pushing plasma televisions in rafts and boats from the stores to their home. There were reports of wide scale looting of non-essential goods and many reports of violent crimes, especially against women. Even people that were evacuated to a "safe location" found themselves victims of these crimes for nearly a week before help arrived. All of these individuals had more than enough warning of the coming storm.

Not all disasters come with a warning. The tsunami that hit Sumatra in 2004 came without much warning at all and killed over 200,000 people. In an instance like this your survival training and preparation could give you just the amount of edge you need to survive. As you prepare and train, you put yourself through mental exercises that will speed your reaction times and allow you to think more rationally in high pressure situations. Not all disasters and events will force you into a survival mode at your PSS, but you still may have to call on your BoB and your plans and preparations.

Let's list some of the more likely and "not as likely" events that you could be looking at in the next 10 years.

Quite Likely

1. Tornado/Hurricane/Blizzard/Flood – All fairly regular weather events in various parts of the country.

2. Hurricane – Certainly fairly regular in some parts of the country.

3. Extended power outage – We will be seeing more of these in the near future; summer and winter outages could get nasty.

4. Chemical Spills / Gas Release – Whether by train derailment, tank rupture, line failure or any other means these events can certainly force you into contingency mode.

5. Terrorist Attack – It could happen at any time, anywhere.

6. Social Disruption – Lots of major issues could cause a breakdown of society as we know it in this country. It could happen tomorrow, or never at all. The bad thing is it seems more likely than not these days.

7. Global Flu Pandemic – We narrowly missed this one in 2009. I think we'll see a bigger one in the next decade. Permafrost is melting around the globe and old bugs that have been dormant for a long ass time are waking up. We don't have immunity to these boys because they got locked in the ice well before humans were wandering around. If an old one doesn't get us, new ones are coming along each day due to mutations.

Spin, Aim, Click….Spin, Aim, Click….Spin, Aim….

Not As Likely

1. Super Volcano Eruption (Yellowstone) – This one happens every 600K years roughly and the last one was roughly 640K years ago. This is a planet changer.

2. Mega Tsunami – The Cumbre Vieja volcano on the island of La Palma in the Canary Islands could potentially send a wall of water at the east coast of the USA at any moment. The volcano is causing the island to fracture and an eruption could send over 20

cubic kilometers of rock sliding to the ocean floor 4 miles below, creating an underwater wave estimated to be 2000 feet tall. Although this is all estimation…I wouldn't be taking any chances.

3. Asteroid Impact – Currently there are no known threats coming at our planet, known meaning that the general public is aware of it. Something tells me that the government would probably hold out on letting us know for a while. Impact could mean nothing to you, or it could destroy the planet, or anything in between.

4. ARkStorm (Atmospheric River 1000 Storm) – Mainly for residents of California this hypothetical but scientifically plausible event would be reminiscent of Noah and the Ark. We're talking over 40 days of rain and storms at 2 inches per hour rainfall levels. Basically people in the path of this storm would think the world was ending.

5. Mega Quake – New Madrid residents, this one's for you. If you live in the Midwest near the New Madrid fault, there could be a whole lot of shakin goin on. The next big one here could be really ugly.

6. Solar Blast CME – How about a burst of energy from the sun that sizzles the USA's power grid into oblivion? Can you say 15 years of living in the dark? That means lots of bad things. The power grid is pretty weak, it's almost like we're daring the sun to do it.

7. Climate Shift – Unlike "Global Warming" and "Climate Change", a Climate Shift occurs over a very short duration of time, estimates vary from a decade to even shorter periods. There is evidence in nature of this occurring at multiple times throughout history.

8. Dec 21, 2012 – No one knows what this one will bring, some people think it's nothing; others are banking their lives on it. I think we'll see a lot of people lose their freaking minds in the months ahead of this date. It might be a good idea to have your plans firmed up prior to this one.

So there you are, just a few of the many things that could happen in the next 10 years or so. This doesn't include black holes, planet X, aliens, nuclear war, gamma ray bursts or any of the other 27 million ways we could all suffer or die.

Just remember, preparing never hurt anyone. Failing to prepare has killed millions and more.

The Real Apocalypse

Sooner or Later

Although a zombie apocalypse is fun to plan and prepare for it is most likely never going to happen. As you read earlier, there are plenty of alternative "End of the World" scenarios. Although you may not get to experience the joy of blasting undead meat bags away with your assault rifle, you could still get plenty of opportunities to play survivor-man.

Obviously there are a few scenarios that don't include humans in the aftermath such a black holes, gamma ray bursts, an exploding sun and more. These scenarios suck, but we won't be here to worry about it. For the scenarios that do include survival of the human race, here are my ideas.

Root Cause

I believe the root cause of the collapse of the human civilization will be Climate Change. Although I do believe we are responsible as humans for hastening this process, I don't believe that we are the base cause of it. Science has shown time and again that nearly everything in the universe works in cycles. The Earth is no different. Current scientific data shows that this planet alternately warms and cools over time in a distinct and predictable pattern.

For the past 10,000 years this planet has enjoyed a period of relative warmth referred to as the Holocene era. During this period climate and weather patterns have been extremely mild in comparison to what scientists believe has occurred in prior eras.

This peace will not last however, and we may be seeing the end of it as we look out of our windows today. The number and magnitude of major storms are increasing and we are seeing increased earthquake activity worldwide according to many other scientists. I am not throwing my hat in as a "true believer" to all of these theories, but I am also not trained in those areas and cannot dispute them. I choose instead to approach with a cautious but open mind. I prepare.

So if things continue, and our planet keeps warming and the ice keeps melting and climate change does in fact raise its ugly head; what will the end result look like?

Air is Rare

Before too long the air on this planet is going to be so full of pollutants it won't be safe to breathe for long periods at a time. We already see this in parts of China and even to some extent in San Diego, CA. I see a future where masks are not only prominent, they are necessary. Prior to the collapse of civilization as we know it the air will already be bad, so hopefully companies will be developing smaller and more efficient personal masks before all hell breaks loose.

The lack of oxygen or addition of other non-breathable chemicals and pollutants in the air may cause defects in people over time. Be prepared for mutations due to radiation if the ozone layer gets too far depleted. Clothing will most likely mirror that of today's desert dwelling nomads, being loose fitting and covering the whole body.

Don't get me wrong, I am not saying that the things we are putting into the air are going to cause all of this. Remember that as the ice and permafrost of the earth melt, they release gases that have been trapped for eons. Some of these gases could be pretty nasty. Also, volcanic eruptions, earthquakes and several other geological changes could release gases into the air. These aren't pleasant either and in abundance could cause great harm and grief.

Mobile Society in the Western US

Residents of the western US will most likely become a more nomadic type of society. Lack of resources and changing seasons will require movement in order to survive. When the power grid fails anyone living in or around Phoenix, AZ will need to leave during summer months, or they will most likely die. As the planet gets hotter due to climate change the ground will become drier and there will be dust storms and wind storms in the western US to rival the famous Dust Bowl. Plants will not grow well in this environment; animals will migrate away from these areas. After a few years these areas will be devoid of humans.

California will continue to be a population center being close to the cooler Pacific air, but the southern regions of that state will quickly lose their luster for most people. Temperate areas such as those near San Francisco will continue to develop.

Washington and Oregon will either become warmer and thus more habitable, or they will suffer deep freezing beyond that which most people will want to endure. This truly depends on the root cause of the "end of the world" scenario. If it is "global warming" then no one really knows what will happen. If the root cause is the cyclic patterns that this planet has been shown to follow, well, people in those areas might want to invest in parkas and pocket hand warmers.

Communal Society in the Midwest US

In the Midwest US you will find more communal societies. Resources will be easier to come by, although still scarce, due to temperature and moisture levels in this region. Large cities will die out and massive amounts of the population will perish as the ability for this planet to support life dwindles.

The survivors will begin coming together into small communities for resource sharing, security and socializing. Travelling families may be welcome to join communities that are not stretched thin on resources, but single travelling men will most likely not be allowed and will be forced to move on.

These small Bible Belt communities will suffer internal strife in the beginning as some choose to follow local law enforcement or government while others turn to religion to show them the way forward. Cooler heads should prevail and if someone in charge has some decent common sense and a little survival training, these communities should prosper with relative ease, if not comfort.

Northern and Northeastern US

The northern and northeastern areas of the US are going to go one of two directions in post climate change times. Either they will be frigidly cold areas constantly receiving arctic temperature winds and massive amounts of snow, or they will be mildly cool to nicely warm areas with lush vegetation. Caution would lead me to avoid the area until the effects of climate change are more widely understood.

If temperatures in these regions plummet and remain there the majority of the year than as you can expect the populations will migrate south. Across most of the US this will not be too big of an issue. Areas south of Chicago will see massive amounts of roaming, starving and cold people heading their way, but the surrounding countryside is quite vast and unpopulated through much of Illinois, Indiana and even Iowa and Ohio, so this should be sustainable as long as they keep moving. You won't want to be in their path though as they will most likely clear the entire area of all resources and certainly crimes against other people will occur in large numbers.

In the northeast there will be huge numbers of people migrating south, and this is going to cause some very large issues. The population density in these areas is such that any increase or nomadic transfer is going to wreak havoc on the local resources.

Appendix A

Survival Tips and Tricks

This guide is not meant as a handbook to living off the land. Unfortunately many people will read this book thinking that I am going to teach them how to build fires, purify water, build a solar power collector or kill a bear with a pocketknife a rubber band and a pair of chopsticks.

In the hope that I can dissuade people from thrashing me publicly, I am going to use this section to cover some basic survival technique instructions. (No, I am not going to teach you to kill a bear with a pocketknife, rubber band and a pair of chopsticks).

Primitive Fire Building

Primitive fire making is not quick or easy. If you run out of modern day materials, this may be your last resort. There are several different methods of doing this, none of which are going to make you giggle for joy.

You will need the following items:

- Spindle – This is a stick that you spin back and forth to create friction on the fireboard

- Fireboard – This is a flat piece of wood used as the base for the Spindle to create heat on

- Tinder – This is DRY material that is flammable

- Patience – This may take a while

- Mandurance – Good luck, Chief

If you create enough friction between the spindle and the fireboard, you can create an ember that can be used to create a fire. Before you can use wood to start a friction based fire, the wood must be very dry. If the wood isn't dry, you'll have to dry it out first.

The Hand Drill

Ready to claim your Man Card? Build a fire to cook on using this method and strut just a little more when you walk. Here are some instructions.

Build a tinder nest. Dry grass, leaves and bark are good materials for this part of the process. Make a small, neat pile and ensure the surrounding area is clear of debris. Have more material nearby in case you succeed!

Cut a v-shaped notch into your fire board and make a small depression adjacent to it.

The bark will be used to catch an ember from the friction between the spindle and fireboard.

Place the spindle into the depression on your fire board. Your spindle should be about 2 feet long for this to work properly. Maintain pressure on the board and start rolling the spindle between your hands, running them quickly down the spindle. Keep doing this until an ember is formed on the fireboard.

Once you see a glowing ember, tap the fire board to drop your ember onto the piece of bark. Transfer the bark to your nest of tinder. Gently blow on it to start your flame.

Finding Water

When you are living off the land, finding water is sometimes not very easy. Depending on where you are and what time of year it is, here are some methods you can use to gather water.

Collect Dew

Take off your cotton shirt and tie it to your ankles. Slowly walk through the dew covered grass, allowing your shirt to absorb the water. Wring out the shirt and repeat.

Many larger leafed plants will collect dew in the mornings. Make sure to check those big broad leaves to see if they have any water on them.

Snow and Ice

Do NOT eat snow or ice without melting them. Eating them in their frozen state can lower your core body temperature and lead to dehydration.

On the Beach

If you are on or near a beach you can try digging behind the sand dunes. Generally water is 1-3 meters deep.

Also, fill a pot with seawater and then drop heated rocks into it, causing steam. Catch the steam in a cloth and then ring it out to have fresh water.

See the Signs

Look for low lying areas or valleys, generally these are created by a water source. Watch for circling birds, or areas that appear to contain more greenery than the surrounding area. Also watch for the convergence of animal tracks. Most animals avoid each other, so a convergence means there is something worthwhile nearby. These are all signs of possible water sources.

Water Filtering

NOTE: You should read a lot more about this subject before drinking water from an unknown source using this technique. I employ the use of boiling and purification tablets when possible in addition to this.

Water is without a doubt the most important thing you will need in a survival situation. There are MANY ways to handle filtering your water for drinking. Remember, filtering and purifying are NOT the same thing. Here's what you will need:

- Two 5 gallon buckets

- One spigot (on/off capable)

- Charcoal

- Sand

- Gravel

- Mesh Screen (door screen will work)

- Tools to cut your buckets

Label your buckets as follows: RAW WATER and FILTERED WATER

Wash all materials, including charcoal and gravel, before building the filter system.

FILTERED WATER BUCKET - Take the Spigot and install it approximately 1/2 inch above the bucket's bottom rim.

RAW WATER BUCKET –

- Cut 5 holes in the bottom of this bucket. Each hole should be about 2 inches in diameter.

- Cut two pieces of screen mesh to fit inside the bucket and place them on the bottom.

- Pour about 3 inches of course sand into the bottom of the bucket. Level it out and ensure it is not leaking through the mesh. If it is leaking through, remove all materials and add another mesh layer. Repeat adding mesh layers until sand does not leak.

- Pour water into the bucket to ensure that it comes all the way through the holes in the bottom.

- Add a 3 inch thick layer of finely crushed charcoal on top of the sand. Test water flow.

- Add a 3 inch layer of crushed gravel on top of the charcoal. Test water flow.

- Place a single layer of mesh on top of the gravel and then repeat the layers of sand, charcoal and gravel again, testing for water throughput each time.

When the bucket is completed you will place the RAW WATER bucket on top of the FILTERED WATER bucket. Place the buckets in an area where you can access both the top of the bucket set and the spigot at the bottom without issue.

Pour raw water into the top bucket and it will filter as it makes its way through the different material layers. The process should take a few moments as the filtering materials slow the speed of the water. Once the water is in the lower bucket, you can use the spigot to extract the water from the system.

NOTE: You will STILL need to purify the water through other means. Filtering only removes the large objects in the water it does not clean the water of bacteria, virus or anything else. I suggest boiling all water that comes from a homemade filtering system. Also, the water may or may not be clear. Get used to drinking stuff that doesn't look tasty. Clean your materials and change out your filtering medium weekly if possible.

NOTE: Replacing the wire mesh with some form of cheesecloth would be fantastic if you have it available. I only use wire mesh in my examples because it is readily available in most cases.

If you are truly living off the land, you are just going to have to take your chances. Try to find a water source that is not stagnant. Flowing water is likely to be much cleaner than stagnant water. If you can locate the water at its source, you may be able to reasonably assume it purity or cleanliness.

Snaring a Meal

Hunger is one thing that you can't avoid. Edible plants aren't always available, although knowing what they are or having a reference book for them is a great idea. Sooner or later you will need something more substantial in your stomach if you are going to continue to survive.

Snaring small animals for food is something that is not too terribly difficult as long as you don't mind killing little fuzzies to eat. Learning to track them is much harder, but there are guides out there for that.

To construct a basic snare you need to create a strangle snare noose out of whatever corded material you have available. I choose this type of snare because instead of simply holding the animal in place, it will kill the animal without my intervention in most cases. Thin material such as twine or clothesline would work well.

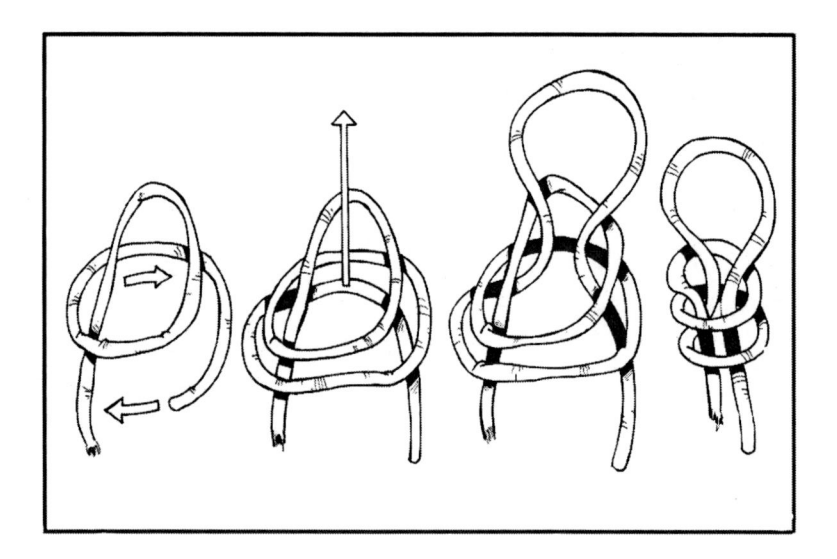

As you can see from the picture above, building the snare is not difficult.

Spread the loop of the snare over an area known to be travelled by the animal you are intending to eat, or at the mouth of an animal den. Spread the noose out enough that the animal does not see it, but not so much that the animal runs through it. Hold the loop open with blades of grass or anything else that won't impede snaring the animal. This type of snare will tighten on the animal the more it struggles to free itself, without intervention the animal should suffocate.

Tie the end of the snare rope to a secure tree or root and walk away. Hopefully before too long you'll have dinner ready and waiting for you.

Keep Your Gas Tank ½ Full

If you feel there is a decent possibility of having to break for your PSS, or just in general if you are cautious, keep at least half a tank of gas in your vehicle. If an emergency happens you may not have time to stop and fill up on your way to wherever you are going. It's also possible that even if you had the time, there may not be any gas to be had.

Get Gas from a Vehicle

In a post-apocalyptic world cars and generators will still run on gas, and it may not be readily available. Finding gas may become increasingly difficult and you may have to resort to less commons sources. In the meantime, work on your methods for extracting gas from vehicles.

Most people think they'll use a syphon hose and suck all the gas out of a car, but that's extremely time consuming, places you in the open for a increased amount of time and it is rather dangerous.

Instead, use a sharpened brass rod or non-sparking punch and a mallet to punch a hole in the bottom of the car's gas tank and slide a plastic container under there to catch the gas as it comes out. This method is certainly no good for the vehicle you are stealing the gas from, but that shouldn't really be your concern. The goals are getting gas and staying alive.

Sleeping on the Run

If you find yourself outside for the night, and building a fire is not a possibility, don't just find yourself a flat spot and curl up for the night. Sleeping on the ground could potentially cause you to lose too much body heat if the ground temperature is colder than your body temperature. Instead, find something to sleep on such as bedding material like pine needles or leaves. If these aren't available try to locate a log or something to put between yourself and the ground.

Add Meat and Chicken to Your Diet

If you find yourself living at your PSS due to an event keep in mind that chickens are pretty hearty little animals that don't require much care. Building a coup is not a lot of work to go through in order to have some eggs for breakfast or a chicken dinner every now and then.

Sheep are also quite useful. If you know how or care to learn, their wool can be used to make extremely nice warm clothing, or if you take the easier route, nice warm blankets and covers. Plus, they don't taste too bad and they eat grass for the most part. Add a few goats into the mix and you have a source for milk without dealing with huge cows.

Preventive Maintenance

I touched on this earlier, but preventive maintenance is very important. Anything can break, but most things only break when you really need them. Learn to properly maintain the important items and make sure you go through some maintenance on these items regularly. Try to keep the proper oils and greases in stock, at least enough for a year of service, in order to ensure proper operation of these items.

Super Glue for Cuts

If you find yourself without a bandage to cover a shallow cut, try super glue. Make sure to wash the cut out and then dry it lightly. Once that's done hold the cut closed and apply super glue back and forth across the wound. It dries very quickly and will hold the cut closed until you can get further attention. In a pinch you can use duct tape, but taking the tape off generally serves to undo the good the tape was doing, and potentially makes things worse.

Cauterize a Wound using a Bullet

*NOT RECOMMENDED AT ALL

Made famous in the 80's when this method of self-cauterization of a wound was shown in a massively famous movie, it will work to stop bleeding. All you need to do is remove the bullet from the shell (carefully of course), and pour the gunpowder from inside the shell onto the wound. Get yourself a match and light that baby up. The more gunpowder you use, the bigger the flame and the more likely you will set yourself on fire. Although minimally effective it should get you through long enough to see a professional without bleeding out, but remember, if the wound is serious you are most likely still bleeding inside, and cauterizing the wound may actually lessen the ability for someone to treat your wound effectively. Currently there are much more effective methods and first aid options for staunching the flow of blood from a wound. Invest in them and you'll be much better off.

Make Soap from Animal Fat

Extract the grease from animal fat by cutting the fat into small pieces and cooking it in a pot. Add a small amount of water so that the fat doesn't stick to the pot while it is cooking. Stir the fat frequently until it is completely rendered (liquid), then pour into a container and allow to harden.

Take ashes from a cooking fire and add a small amount of water to them. This mixture (slurry) becomes the abrasive for your soap.

In a cooking pot, mix two parts grease to one part slurry and boil until the mixture thickens. When the soap is thickened, pour it into a pan to harden. Once the soap is hardened you can cut it into bars. You can also use it in liquid form if you want to do so.

Don't Kill Yourself

Dehydration

Know the signs of dehydration and understand them.

- 2% dehydration –Thirsty
- 5% dehydration –Tired and hot. Strength and Endurance decrease.
- 10% dehydration – Delirium and blurred vision
- 20% dehydration – Death

Physical symptoms of dehydration include:

- Dark urine with foul odor
- Decreased urine output
- Dark or Sunken eyes
- Fatigue
- Emotional instability
- Loss of skin elasticity
- Trench line in center of tongue

Things NOT to drink when you are dehydrated:

- Alcoholic beverages – Dehydrate you further and impair judgment
- Urine – Contains harmful waste products and is 2% salt
- Blood – Blood is considered a food and requires more water to digest, not to mention it is unhealthy
- Saltwater – Saltwater (Ocean) is about 4% salt. Drinking this causes further dehydration as well as other problems

Cook Your Food Thoroughly

Make sure to remember that eating wild animals is much different than eating farm bred or slaughtered animals. The animals you kill and eat in the woods will not have the benefit of a medicated or enhanced diet and they will most likely have fleas or other parasitic creatures living on them or in them.

Cooking your food until it's hot won't necessarily kill all of the little nasties you could encounter. You need to ensure that everything is cooked very thoroughly and for a long period of time. If you have survived the zombie apocalypse, being taken down by a gut bug is really going to be messed up.

Boil Your Water

Unless you have a very large supply of purification tablets or you know for certain your water is good to go, you will need to boil it. Dirty water can kill you just as easily as zombies can.

Filtering your water is not the same as purifying. Filtering does not get rid of bacteria or viruses. Make sure you don't forget this, it is very important.

Aim for the Head....NOT!

Don't waste time or bullets aiming for the head of your zombie attacker. Chances are that infected/zombie attackers will be just as impervious to bullets as normal people. If you CAN hit them in the head without wasting time and ammo, knock yourself out, otherwise it's just going to give them more time to get you while you waste valuable resources.

Guns are Dangerous

If you choose to arm yourself with firearms, remember that they are extremely dangerous. Learn to use them properly and never forget how much respect they demand. Forgetting these lessons for even a split second can ruin lives.

Eco Living

A famous frog once lamented about the difficulties of being green. It certainly ain't easy and it can be downright dangerous if you don't know how to do it properly. Whether you are talking about eating certain foods to maintain a green diet or creating your own renewable energy there are serious dangers involved. LEARN about these things before you try them.

Appendix B

Statistical Data

Per FEMA's U.S. Fire Administration:

- An estimated 374,900 residential building fires are reported to U.S. fire departments each year and cause an estimated 2,630 deaths.

Per the National Flood Insurance Program website:

- Floods are the #1 most common natural disaster in the United States.
- Floods and flash floods happen in all 50 states.

Per the National Oceanic and Atmospheric Administration:

- The current average lead-time for tornado warnings is 13 minutes.
- Approximately 1,200 tornadoes hit the U.S. each year.
- Tornadoes can occur in any state in the U.S.

Per various Internet flu resources:

- London's Great Plague killed 100,000 people (1665-1666)
- The Great Plague of Marseilles killed 100,000 people (1720)
- The Moscow Plague and riot killed up to 200,000 people (1771)
- The Russian Flu killed up to 1,000,000 people (1890-1891)
- The Hong Kong Flu killed 1,000,000 people (1968)
- The Third Cholera Epidemic in Russia killed 1,000,000 people (1852-1859)
- The Antonine Plague killed roughly 6.5 million people (AD 165-AD 180)
- The Plague of Justinian killed 25 million people (AD 541)
- The Spanish Flu (H1N1) killed an estimated 40-75 million people (1918)
- The Black Death killed 100 million people, 60% of Europe's population (1348-1350)

Appendix C

Links and Info

Below, please find some of the more prominent places to seek information and about planning and preparation. Although my opinions differ from some of those you will read, I feel it is best to provide all manner of information and advice and allow you, the reader, to determine what is best for you to utilize.

Centers for Disease Control and Prevention (CDC)

www.cdc.gov

Federal Emergency Management Agency (FEMA)

www.fema.gov

(The FEMA website contains links to several other very well developed and maintained sites with quite a bit of information)

Zombie Games:

To break up the monotony of surviving in a post zombie apocalypse world, it will be necessary to find joy and happiness in as much as possible. With that in mind, and because some things just have to be tried at least once, we introduce Zombie Games. These are ideas on good ways to utilize your undead neighbors and friends in ways that will help break up the day and bring a little sunshine into an otherwise gloomy existence.

ZomB Bowling:

This game is only possible if your breed of zombie is the slow, shuffling sort. Fast zombies will ruin the fun and force you to destroy them before everyone gets a turn.

To play ZomB Bowling you need to find a street on a hill. Retrieve the smallest car you can find and park it at the top of the hill. Leave the door open, the key turned and the vehicle in neutral with the parking brake on. The current player will run around the area gathering zombies in a pack. Once he/she has secured what they feel is an adequate number of zombies, the player leads them to the center of the street. The player will then run up the center of the street as fast as possible, jump in the car and release the parking brake, aiming the car into the zombie pack. After the car hits the pack you get 1 point for each zombie that can no longer stand, and 2 points for any zombie destroyed. Style points can be added for the gathering run and impact.

ZomB Jarts:

ZomB Jarts is a spin-off of the old Lawn Jarts game. The Jarts themselves may need to be handmade, as I don't believe they are sold publicly any longer. Each player's Jarts should be easily recognizable as their own. This game is suitable only for slow, shuffling zombies.

To play ZomB Jarts each player will be issued 3 Jarts. Jarts are oversized metal darts with sharp points. Players will gather area zombies into a large group and lead them to a designated area. Once the zombies are in the proper position, the players will throw their Jarts utilizing a long, underhand motion. Jarts should be thrown no less than 20 feet into the air for maximum affect. After the Jarts land, scoring is as follows:

1 Point – Jart impales Zombie anywhere except head

2 Points – Jart impales Zombie in head

3 Points – Jart impales Zombie in head and destroys It

No points are awarded for Jarts that do not impale a Zombie

Whack-A-ZomB:

Whack-A-ZomB is a game of grace, speed and balance. To play Whack-A-Zomb you will need a large hole, roughly 15 feet in diameter and approximately 5-6 feet deep. Gather several zombies and lead them into the hole. The player will then have 1 minute to whack as many zombies as possible while keeping them from escaping the hole. One point is awarded for each successful whack. Double whacking a single zombie without an intervening whack on another zombie will result in only one point being scored.

Jamie Mathieson – The Illustrator

Finding the proper illustrator for this book was not easy. Luckily I found Jamie Mathieson in only a few months of searching and we were able to connect and complete this project.

Working with Jamie has been wonderful. I was concerned that I would have to "settle" for an artist's interpretation of my book, but instead I found someone with the ability to understand my descriptions and literally transpose my thoughts to paper.

I hope that I have the opportunity to work with Jamie on future projects, as this project has run extremely well.

Please take the time to view more of Jamie's work on the following pages and also by following his contact information, which is also provided.

Jamie Mathieson - Bio

Jamie Mathieson was born in Toronto, Ontario Canada. From an early age he was an avid comic reader and artist. It was his fondness for comics that led Jamie to attend art classes at the A.G.O. as young as eight years old.

At fourteen Jamie moved to Vancouver and continued with his studies at the Academy of Art and renowned Emily Carr University of art and design. It was from there Jamie attended the Vancouver Film School and graduated with a degree in classical animation and a movie that was showcased at the famous Spike and Mike International Film festival titled "**ALCOHOLICAT**". Other projects Jamie has worked on is the comic book series **LINE COOKS, OLDFOLKS** and **THE ARTIST AND THE ALIEN**.

Jamie's respect and appreciation for the comic medium led to his collaboration with Alex Newton on this tale of post apocalyptic zombie carnage and survival.

Jamie is a graphic artist who currently resides in Vancouver Canada.

To view his online portfolio please got: www.jamiemathiesonart.com

Or contact him at johnnystarband@hotmail.com

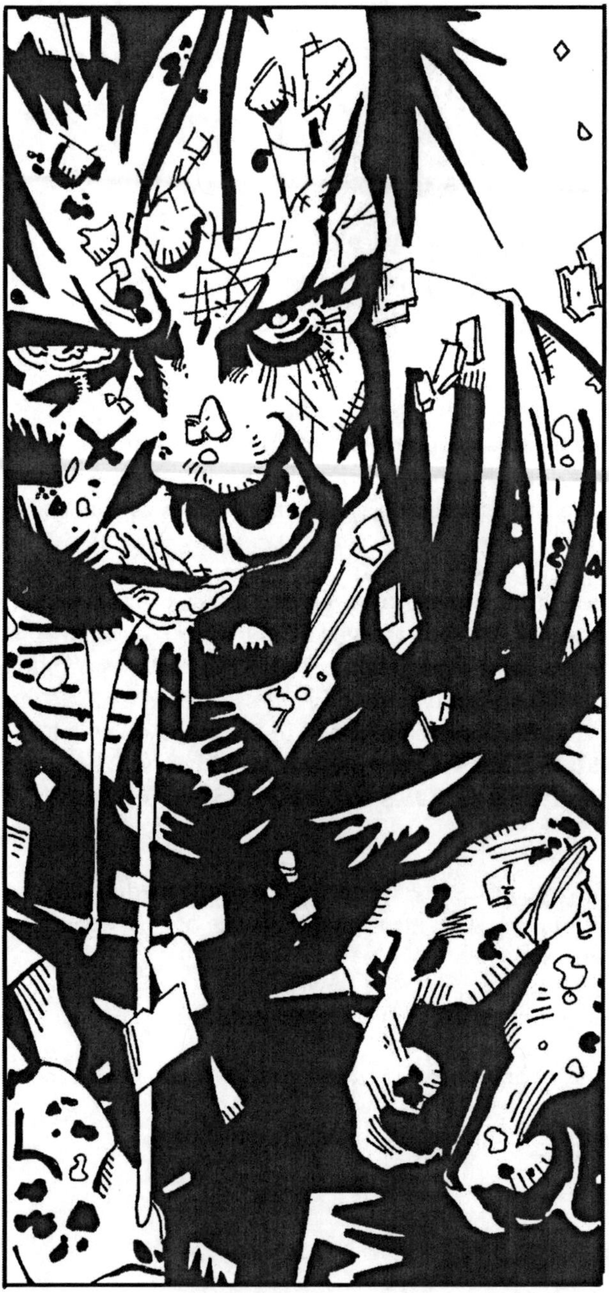

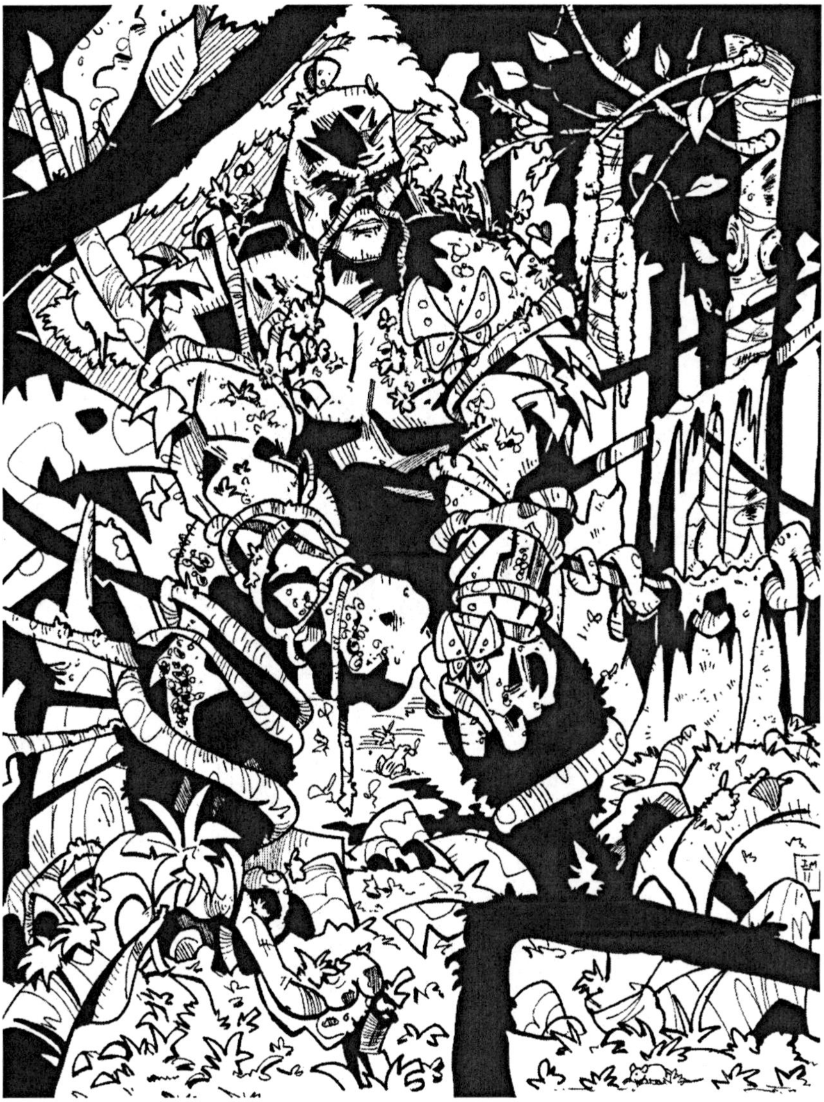

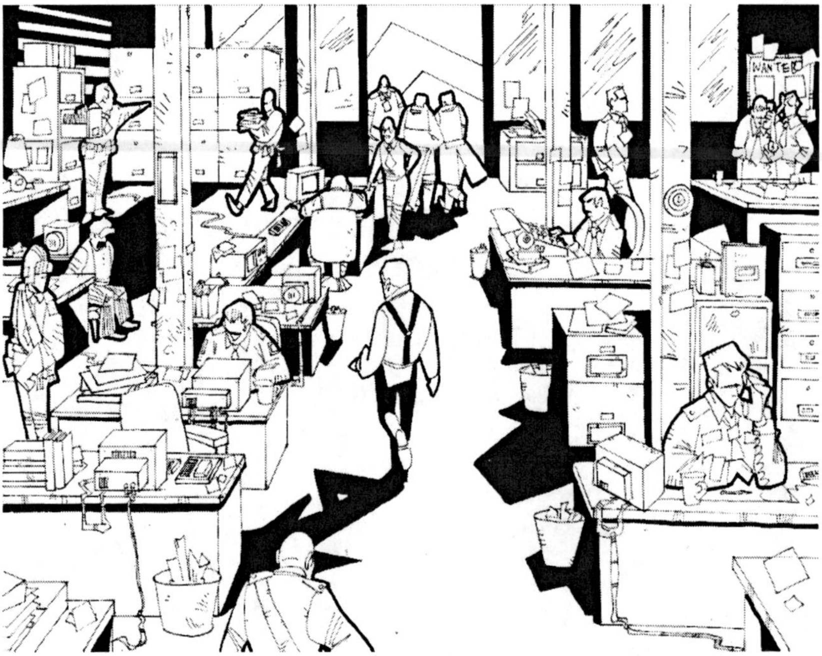
WANTED

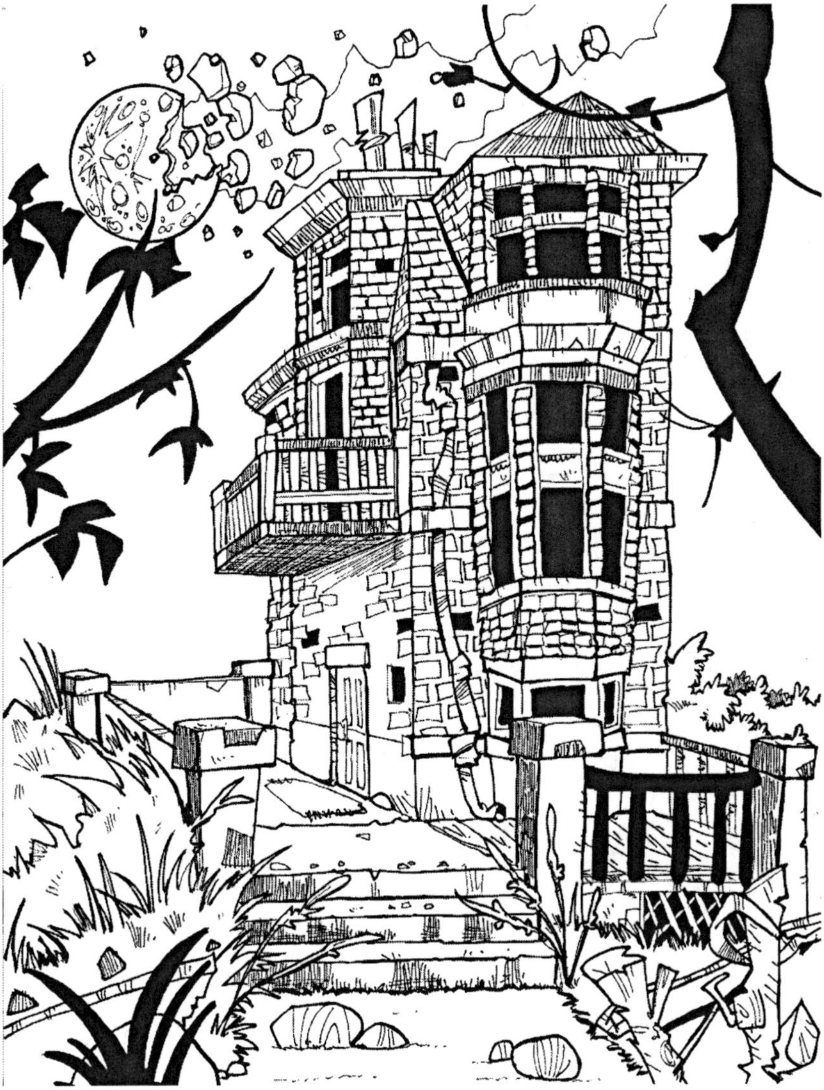

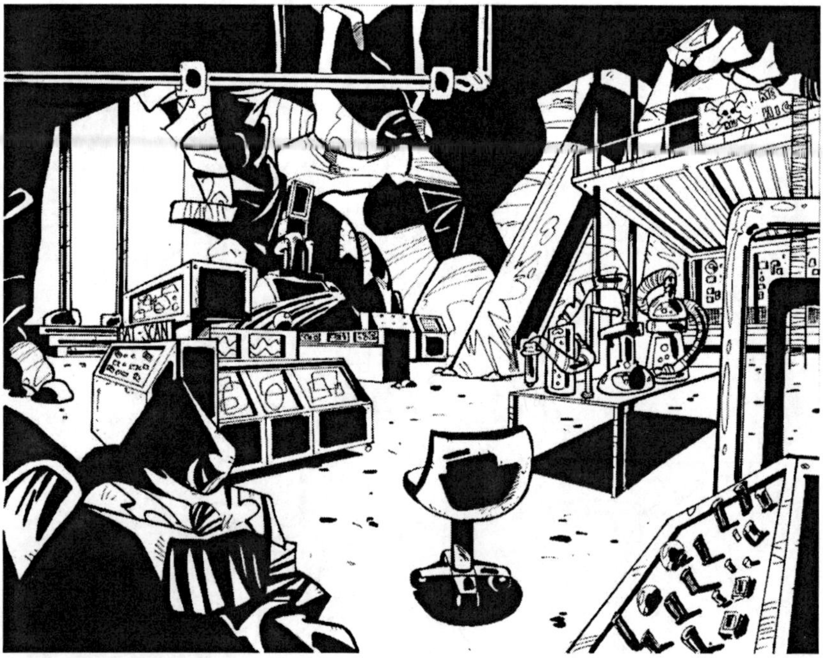
BAT-SCAN

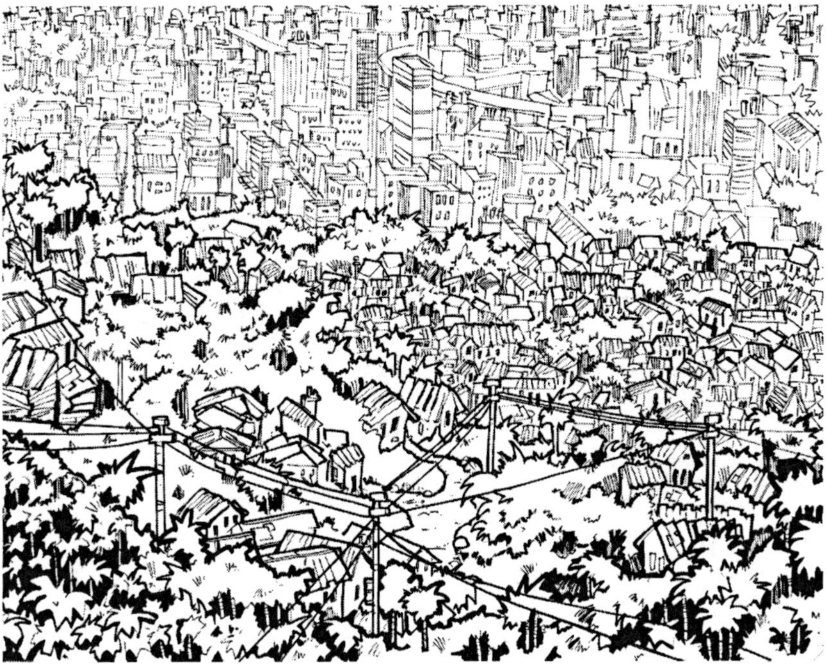

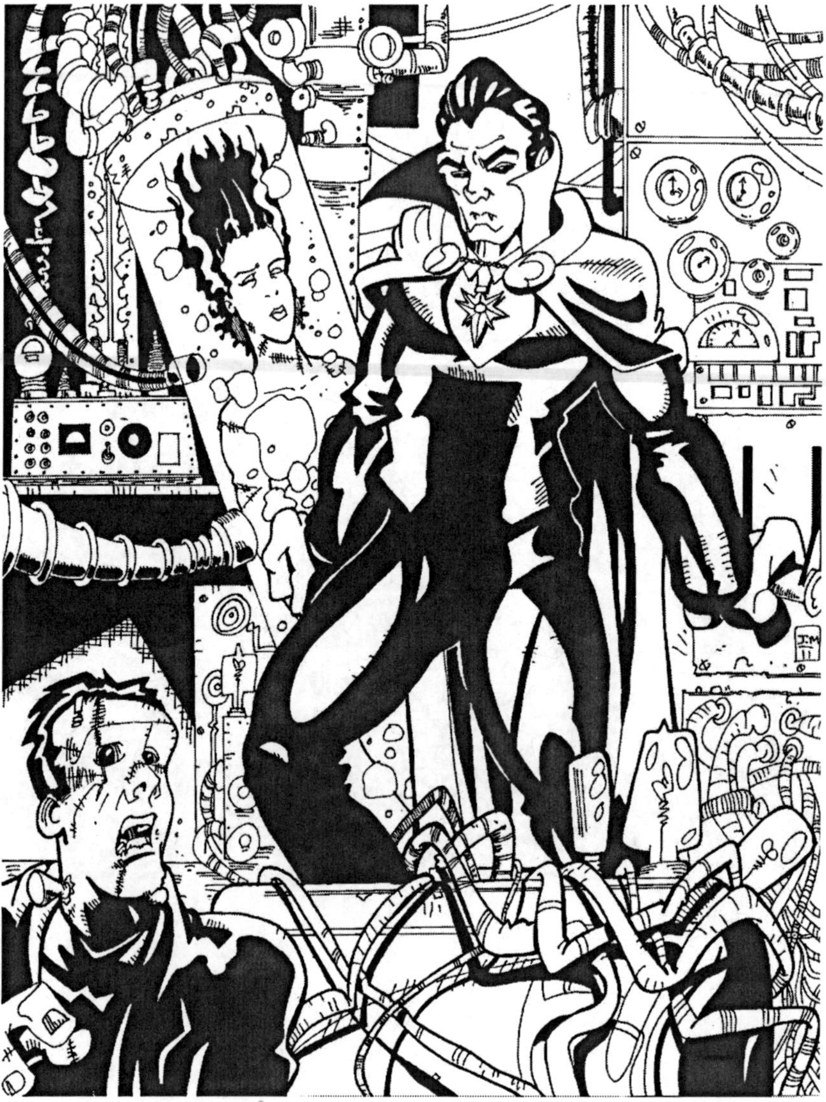

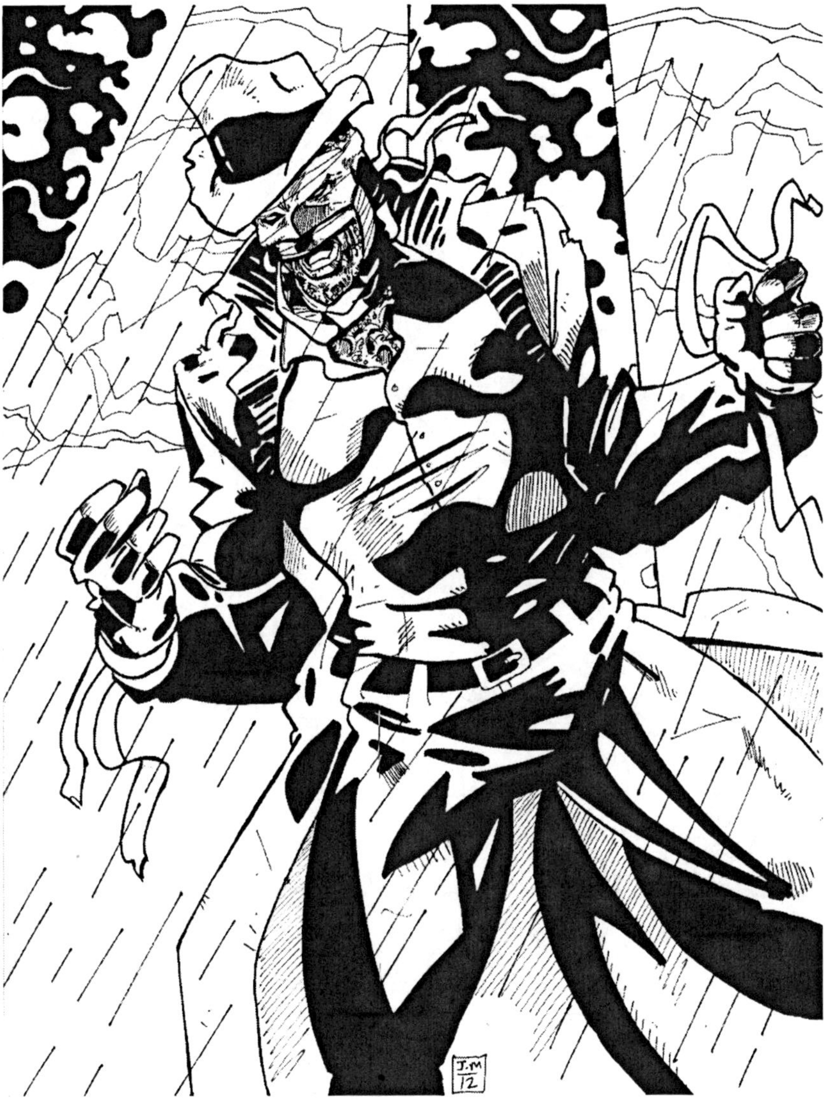
J.M
12

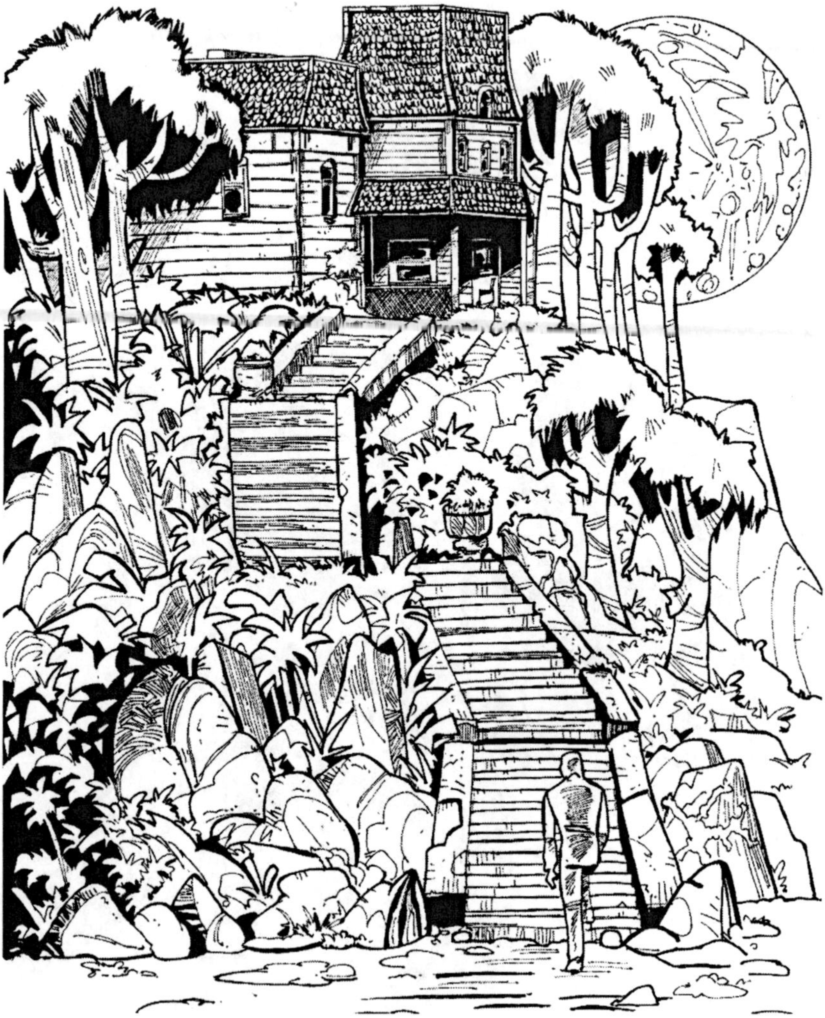

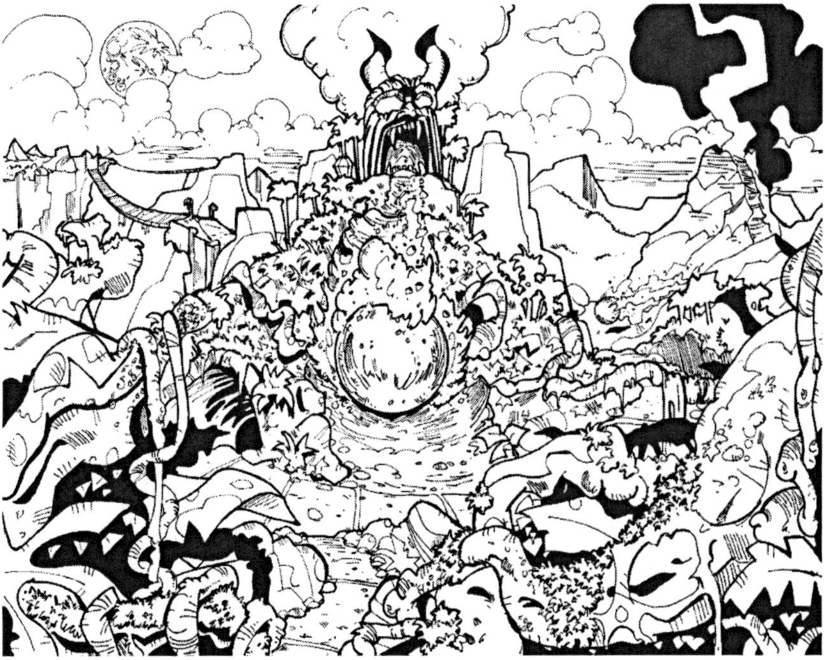

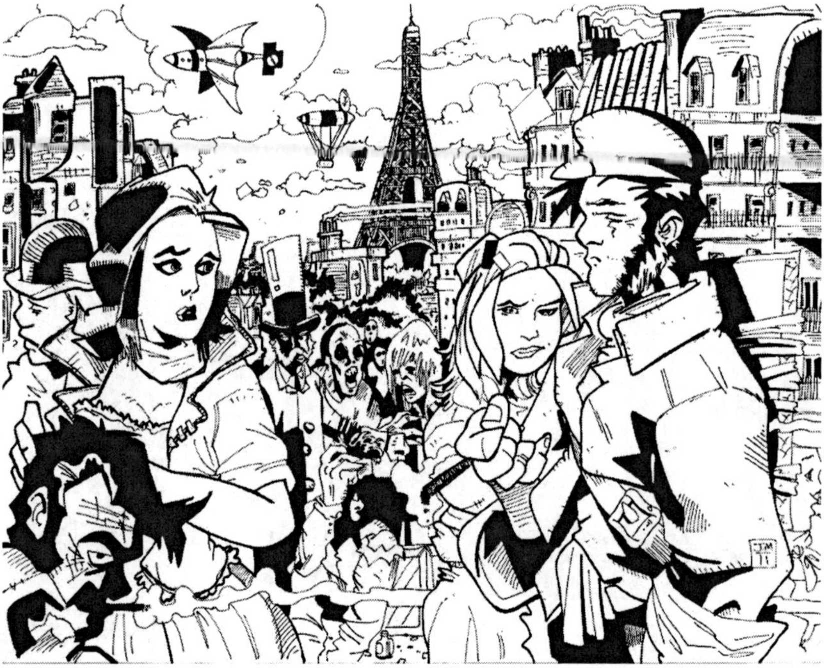

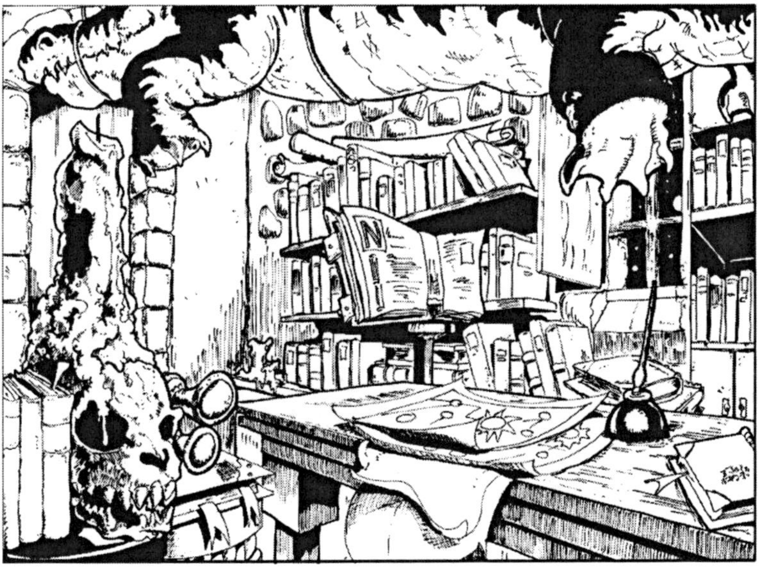

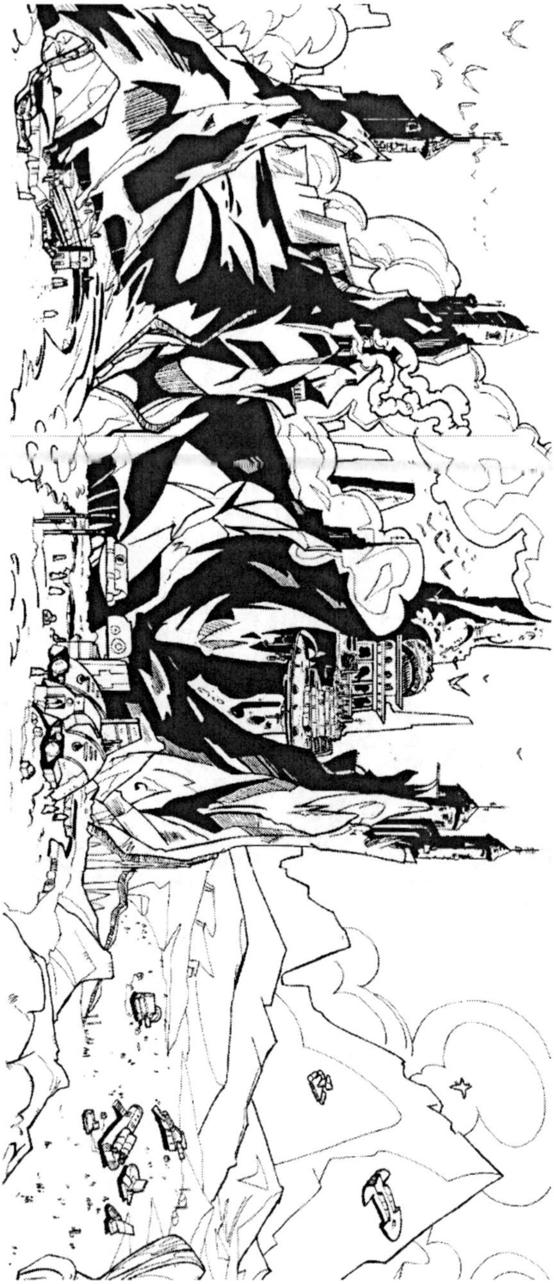